I0764640

Formal Salutations
New & Selected Poems

FORMAL SALUTATIONS
NEW & SELECTED POEMS

by

William Baer

Measure Press
Evansville, Indiana

Printed in the United States of America
First Edition

The text of this book is composed in Baskerville.
Composition by R.G.
Manufacturing by Ingram.

Baer, William
Formal Salutations: New and Selected Poems / by William Baer — 1st ed.

ISBN-13: 978-1-939574-26-8
ISBN-10: 1-939574-26-9
Library of Congress Control Number: 2018946925

Measure Press
526 S. Lincoln Park Dr.
Evansville, IN 47714
http://www.measurepress.com/measure/

Acknowledgments:

The author wishes to thank the editors of the publications in which these new poems have appeared, sometimes in slightly different form.

"Portugal," "Carmen CI," and "Autopyschography" appeared in *Able Muse*. "The Scientist of the Mind" appeared in *Acumen*. "The Artist of Fashion" and "The Poet Moderne" appeared in *Art Ideas*. "Texas" appeared in *Atlanta Review*. "December" appeared in *First Things*. "Poem on the Lam" and "The History of Western Poetry" appeared in *Light*. "On His Blindness" appeared in *The London Magazine*. "Paolo and Francesca" appeared in *Modern Age*. "To an Old Poet" appeared in *New Letters*. "Bobblehead" and "Demolition Derby" appeared in *The Orchards*. "The Journalist of Reputation" appeared in *Piedmont Literary Review*. "The Playwright of the People" appeared in *Plains Poetry Journal*. "A Poet of the 13th Century" appeared in *Poetry Salzburg Review*. "Portrait" appeared in *Presence*. "The Abbé of the Avant-garde" appeared in *The Remnant*. "New Jersey Noir" appeared in *Trajectory*. "The Philosopher of Action" appeared in *University Bookman*. "The Stand-In" appeared in *Valparaiso Poetry Review*. "The Ballad of Jeanne Bertaut" and "Where in the World is the Girl for Me?" appeared in *Verse-Virtual*.

Earlier poems were published in:

The Unfortunates, Truman State University Press, 1997.
"Borges" and Other Sonnets, Truman State University Press, 2003.
Luís de Camões: Selected Sonnets, The University of Chicago Press, 2005.
The Ballad Rode into Town, Turning Point, 2007.
"Bocage" and Other Sonnets, Texas Review Press, 2008.
Psalter, Truman State University Press, 2011.
Love Sonnets, Kelsay Press, 2015.

For Toni

CONTENTS

I. Formal Salutations

blank verse

New Jersey Noir 1

villanelle

Where in the World is the Girl for Me? 5

sonnets

Poem on the Lam 6
Bobblehead 7
The Stand-In 8
Demolition Derby 9
The Antechamber of Hell 10
The Grammar School V.P. 11

terza rima

Paolo and Francesca 12

parodies

With a Haitian in the Metro 15
Frog 16
Thirteen Ways of Looking at a Black Turd 17
The Red-Haired Poet 18
Arse Poetica 19

translations

Carmen CI *(Catullus)* 20
To a Woman Passing By *(Baudelaire)* 21
Portugal *(Unamuno)* 22
December *(Angelini)* 23
Autopyschography *(Pessoa)* 24
Portrait *(Meireles)* 25

ballad

The Ballad of Jeanne Bertaut 26

couplets
The Abbé of the Avant-garde 29
The Journalist of Reputation 30
The Poet Moderne 31
The Scientist of the Mind 32
The Artist of Fashion 33
The Playwright of the People 34
The Philosopher of Action 35
triolets
Visiting All the Places We Once Made Love 36
Agenda 37
trochees
A Descent into the Maelström 38
anapests
Transgression 39
children's verse
The Little Boy Who Couldn't Rhyme 40
nonsense
Prince Charming 44
little willies
Little Willie 45
translations
Caesar *(Borges)* 46
On his Blindness *(Borges)* 47
A Morning in 1649 *(Borges)* 48
A Poet of the 13th Century *(Borges)* 49
A Soldier of Urbana *(Borges)* 50
Texas *(Borges)* 51
To an Old Poet *(Borges)* 52
quatrain
The History of Western Poetry 53

II. The Unfortunates

Breaking and Entering 57
Hospital 58
Prosecutor 59
Librarian 60
Trauma Center 61
Garbage 62
Confidence Man 63
Runway 66
East River 67
Telephone Psychic 68
Monte Carlo 69
Disphobic 70
Suicide Note 71

III. "Borges" and Other Sonnets

Quarantine 75
Firebrand 76
Lecture 77
The Scream 78
Secret Police 79
Pumpkin 80
Rattler 81
Footnote 82
The Poem 83
Balcony 84
The Odyssey, Book Twenty-Three *(Borges)* 85
The Borges *(Borges)* 86
To Luís de Camões *(Borges)* 87
The Sea *(Borges)* 88

Allusion to the Death of Colonel Francisco Borges (1835–1874) *(Borges)* 89
Snowflake 90
Thief 91
Monster 92
Confession 93
Swimming Pool 94
Conspiracy 95
Last Will 96
Labyrinth 97

IV. Luís de Camões: Selected Sonnets

Curse 101
Shipwreck 102
Dear Gentle Soul 103
Tagus 104
Natércia 105
Escape 106
Exile 107
Sin 108
Nature 109
Refuge 110
Drowned Lover 111
Reader 112

V. The Ballad Rode into Town

The Ballad Rode into Town 115
Amnesiac 118
The Ballad of the Labyrinths 121
The Ballad of the Death-Row Lover 124

VI. "Bocage" and Other Sonnets

Arrhythmia 129
Elevator 130
Cartographer 131
Wanted Poster 132
Fog 133
Intruder 134
Self-Portrait *(Bocage)* 135
Camões *(Bocage)* 136
Inês de Castro *(Bocage)* 137
Letter of Resignation 138
Impersonator 139
Chocolate 140
Protanopia 141
Like a Speeding Bullet 142
The Rain Rains *(Meireles)* 143
Spider Hole *(Meireles)* 144
Coimbra Night *(Meireles)* 145
Cage 146
Bookstore 147
The Shower 148
The Puzzle House 149
Illiterate Love Note 150
The "2" Train 151

VII. Psalter

Snake 155
Pharaoh 156
David 157
Elijah 158

Jezebel 159
Jeremiah 160
Theotokos 161
Egypt 162
Centurion 163
Andrew 164
Love Your Enemies 165
Light of the World 166

VIII. Love Sonnets

Itinerary 169
Island Beach 170
Sappy Love Poem 171
Lying in Bed with Me 172
Bad Girl Sonnet: Redux 173
Bad Girl Sonnet: Hey, Good-Lookin' 174
The Betrayal 175
Dry-Rot 176
Toxicity 177
ICU 178
Embraceable You 179
Turbulence 180
The Swimming Pool Float 181
Meet Me in the Apocalypse 182
Love 183

The Author 185

“But no formal salutation was exchanged.”

— Moby-Dick

I. *Formal Salutations*
(2019)

New Jersey Noir

For Ross Macdonald (r.i.p.)

1.

I was loading my Colt when she walked in the room.
She wore a tight red dress, with Gucci spikes,
and a face that had launched a thousand broken dreams.
Her lips were a shimmering Venus-Flytrap red,
and her dark Hispanic hair tumbled over her shoulders
like the Paterson Falls in a winter thunderstorm.
Her breasts seemed almost anonymous in their perfection,
and I tried not to notice their subtle undulations
with every single breath she took.
Yeah, she was a knock-out, but I'd been knocked-out
too many times to attempt another round.
Her eyes were a soft seductive Hershey brown,
lovely, deep, screwed-up, and on a mission.
She stared at me so deep my insides hurt.
I knew the type. She was *more* than "trouble,"
she was a walking/talking battle-zone,
where many a doomed Custer had made his last stand.
She seemed as though disappointed with *everything*,
even her disappointments. Then she spoke:
"I want you to find my stupid brother," she said.
She was a woman you couldn't say no to.
"No," I said, "I'm buried with stuff right now."
"Unbury yourself, and I'll pay you triple."
I loved the husky echoes in her voice,
and I loved the enticing sound of money.
"Fine," I said, "tell me about your brother."

2.

I didn't have to "find" her stupid brother;
I knew exactly where Eddie was. And why.
So I stopped at Gino's Bails to refresh my memory,
and did some snooping at the Paterson courthouse.
Eddie'd been a screw-up ever since
he'd oozed his way out of his mother's womb.
Like me, he'd always lived in Paterson,
the badass city in the badass state,
founded by a guy named Hamilton,
which seemed an experiment in chaos theory,
a mix of Lord of the Flies, Thunderdome,
Blade Runner, and the wild wild West.
As for Eddie, he was lost in the chaos,
just another hapless Paterson punk;
hell, even his rap sheet was dull and uninteresting.
Back in the day, he'd always steered clear of me,
but I'd knocked him against the wall a couple of times
and cuffed him twice for the Paterson boys-in-blue.

3.

She walked in the room in another tight red dress,
less bare shoulders, with a bit more cleavage,
but the same "holy hell" overall effect.
In her right hand, she was holding a Glock 19,
pointing it over the desk and into my face.
"You find my brother?" she asked rhetorically.
"Yeah, he's watching cartoons in his Sing-Sing cell,
exactly where I put him, on a fifteen-to-twenty,
which you already knew when you hired me."

"Well, aren't you the smart-ass!" she scoffed.
But her eyes were different today. Dead like a bird's.
You ever notice that? Their eyes seem lifeless
even when they're still alive and watching,
as if fronting for some dark unspeakable void.
"I wanted you to think about it," she said,
"before I put a bullet through your brain."
"Look, honey, I knew *exactly* who you were
when you walked through my door yesterday:
the mousey little sister, maybe thirteen,
with the cropped, punked, and bleached-blonde hair,
who sat alone in the back of the courthouse
every single day of Eddie's trial,
when they sent him up on a kiddy rap.
And by the way," I added, "you've cleaned up nicely."
She wasn't flattered. "I hate wiseasses like you."
At seventeen, she'd taken her pick from a lineup
of every Paterson dork with bucks in the bank,
built herself a mansion on Garret Mountain,
divorced the schmuck, burned him in marital court,
then sat in her empty castle, snorting lines,
and, apparently, blaming me for Eddie — and everything.
Why she didn't blame the presiding judge
or the jury foreman, I had no idea.
Maybe, deep down inside, she liked me;
I suppose we could have made a handsome couple.
But not today.

4.

I saw her finger tighten on the trigger,
so I shot her in the leg, from under my desk,

right through the front of my mahogany desk,
right through her pretty calf and into the wall.
I'd never shot a woman before, and maybe
I should have felt bad about it, but I didn't,
although I did hope it wouldn't leave much of a scar.
She crumpled to the floor and her Glock
went flying. She didn't cry or make a sound;
she simply wrapped her arms around her knees
and watched the blood dripping down her leg.
I threw her a handkerchief and called 911.
Sure, I could have made up some cock-and-bull
about how it was all an unfortunate accident,
but I believe in my heart that anyone who tries to kill me
should spend, at least, a year or two in jail.

Where in the World is the Girl for Me?

Where in the world is the girl for me?
Could she be here? Or far away?
Where in the world could she possibly be?

Is she sitting at home watching T.V.,
or dining alone in a Village café?
Where in the world is the girl for me?

Is she floating through dreams on a desolate sea,
tossing in sleep in a damp negligee?
Where in the world can she possibly be?

Is she kind, and thoughtful, sometimes carefree,
loves movies, and poems, and walks by the bay?
Where in the world is the girl for me?

Is she lonely, unattached, and free,
and, sometimes, does she also say:
Where in the world can he possibly be?

Is she sitting alone stirring her tea,
hoping, somehow, I'll find her today?
Where in the world is the girl for me?
Where in the world can she possibly be?

Poem on the Lam

The thing took off about three weeks ago,
then spotted (though the cops don't give a damn)
picking fights at the Cheyenne Rodeo,
then stoned in Vegas, Rio, and Amsterdam.
So what's it really *really* want? Who knows?
In truth, it seemed quite typical of its times,
quite ordinary, another one of those
"Who am I really?" sonnets with silly rhymes.
But now it's "turned itself in" at the Palms Hotel,
flush with uppers, flashing a switchblade knife,
screaming, "Send me back to my 14-walled cell;
I need a little order in my life!"
It seems that even this most recalcitrant poem
has finally decided there's no place like home.

Bobblehead

Last week, I made a bobblehead of you.
Your head's, of course, too big, but all the rest
is you: honey-blonde hair, eyes of blue,
even the pink Armani dress you like the best.
"Would you," I ask, "like to stroll around the lake?
And could we lie together all night long?
Could I make you breakfast whenever you wake,
and rub your feet, and hum your favorite song?
Could you love me till the stars go dead?
And will you meet me *anywhere* in town?"
Ever so gently, I touch the top of your head,
which bobbles up, then down, then up, then down,
as, over and over, you happily acquiesce,
smiling and nodding: yes, yes, yes, yes, yes.

The Stand-In

Sometimes I get absorbed in the leading role,
the public persona that all the others see,
but, mostly, deep in my divided soul,
I'm just a stand-in for whom I'm supposed to be.
But like a good stand-in, I'm right on cue,
I'm always ready, and I always try to please,
I never embellish or add anything new,
and I always try to put the cast at ease.
But unlike other stand-ins, I'm satisfied
and never really covet the leading role,
besides, I know it's not for me to decide,
he's he, I'm me, and it's out of my control.
But, sometimes, I wonder what the others see
and wonder if he's just standing-in for me.

Demolition Derby

Why am I out here getting smacked and slammed
in a useless Corvair with a busted accelerator,
endlessly pummeled and illegally rammed
by a Chrysler Imperial "Devastator,"
as you smash me back-and-forth, and crash,
again and again, my tin-can outer shell,
until there's nothing more of me to smash?
Then you drive away to some other guy's demo hell.
And *no one* who really knew us back in the day,
who'd witnessed the slash-and-burn, the hit-and-run,
would read this demo-analogy and say
that it's unfair, "too much," or over-done.
Even today, I drive with indecision,
fully expecting another blind-side collision.

The Antechamber of Hell

I'm sitting in the antechamber of Hell,
in the cancer clinic's so-called "waiting" room,
with its modern white walls, its antiseptic smell,
and schlock-pop music shrouding the gloom-and-doom.
I thumb through a magazine's old sexposé
about some bimbo star in a low-budget thriller,
while, in the next room, my love's getting chemo today,
as they poison the stuff within her that's trying to kill her.
Later, I'll drive her to our cabin on the lake,
where no one's to blame, where nothing makes any sense,
and while she's sleeping, I'll lie in the dark awake,
thinking: if she survives, I'll fix the fence,
but if she doesn't, I'll spread kerosene around
and burn this place and its memories to the ground.

The Grammar School V.P.

They sit and squirm in my office, one by one,
then tell me their little-kid fears and sinless sins,
and when I've helped them all, and think I'm done,
a ten-year-old blondie strolls in, scoffs, and begins:
"I'm orphaned, with a hyper-low esteem,
and cyber-bullied my only friend today;
I dropped some anthrax in Emmy's vanilla ice cream,
and, beneath my dress, I'm wearing a negligee."
My smarty-pants daughter smiles, and we laugh awhile;
until she admits, "Sometimes, I hate your ex-wife,"
her mother, who wasn't much for self-denial,
who left for California to start a "new" life.
She takes my hand, "It's only *partly* true,
besides, all I really need is you."

Dante

Paolo and Francesca
— *Inferno*, from Canto V

"Could I speak to those two lovers who've sinned,
together, in betrayal and lust, and now appear
to whirl forever, endless, upon the wind?"

"Be ready," Vergil advised, "when they come near,
and call to them as they come whirling through,
and maybe they'll find a way to visit us here."

So when the whirlwinds brought them back in view,
I called out loud, "Lovers, would it be all right,
within your torment, if I could speak with you?"

Immediately, they rose within the hellish night,
like two doves flying homeward towards their nest,
with wings raised up and spread and fixed for flight.

And so they came, abandoning the rest
of Dido's group, to glide on the wind's foul gust,
seduced by the sincerity of my request.

"Still-living creature," she said, "so kind and just,
who's traveled through the rank infernal air
to pity us, who've blackened the world with lust.

If we were still God's friends, we'd offer a prayer
that the King of the Universe might mercifully bestow
His peace on you, who've pitied our despair.

And since the whirling winds now cease to blow,
I'll do whatever you wish, and do my best,
and tell you everything you'd like to know.

I was born in a city on the shoreline's eastern crest,
where the waters of the River Po finally depart
and disperse themselves into their ocean's rest.

But Love had captured my Paolo, and right from the start
my sweet soft flesh was all he was thinking of,
and now that my body's gone, it tears me apart.

Then Love, which exempts no one from the power of love,
offered me Paolo, and I fell under his spell,
and I *still* love him, as I did in the world above.

But Love led to murder, and deep in the depths of Hell,
my husband, who killed us, is, forever, confined."
So I listened to every word she had to tell.

And when she was finished, I fell into a blind
and dark depression and lowered my face,
until Vergil said: "Tell me what's on your mind."

And I said: "What terrible desire to embrace
some sensate love, which seemed both sweet and true,
has led them both to this horrible and hellish place?"

I turned to Francesca: "The pain you're suffering through
rips my sorrowful, weeping heart apart,
and I have nothing but pity for the both of you.

But tell me: When did everything start?
When did Love set your passions free
and reveal the desires hidden within your heart?"

"There's no greater sorrow," she explained to me,
"than remembering happiness while here in pain.
I'm sure that your teacher, Vergil, will agree.

But since you have the desire to ascertain
how everything began, when our passions burned
so out of control, I'll weep as I explain:

One day, for pleasure, we read a book and learned
of Lancelot, how love trapped him within its spell.
At the time, we were alone and unconcerned.

But often, we blushed, as our eyes furtively fell
into each others' seductively, just before
that terrible moment that brought us here to Hell:

When Lancelot kissed the lips he was longing for,
recklessly throwing his inhibitions away,
then Paolo, who's trapped with me forevermore,

Kissed me on the mouth, and I would have to say
that the book and its pandering author magnified
our lusts, and we read nothing more that day."

And while Francesca was speaking, her lover cried,
wailing such a loud and pitiful sound,
I fainted away, as if I'd actually died,

And fell, as a dead body falls to the ground.

With a Haitian in the Metro

(1913)

The juxtaposition of our faces in the crowd;
Nettles in the Tao. (Wow!)

Frog

(1916)

The Frog comes
on little French feet.

It sits looking
over the Chicago Poems
with silent disdain
and then moves on.

Thirteen Ways of Looking at a Black Turd

(1917)

1

Scrapping its innuendos
Off your shoe.

2

From a glass coach
In Connecticut
With the scrawny men of Haddam.

3-13

Being of three minds:
You and your woman and the black turd
Are one.

The Red-Haired Poet

(1923)

so much depends
upon

the red-haired
harrow

smashing the metro-
nomes

amid the literary
chickens.

Arse Poetica

(1926)

A poem should be dumb,
Like its poet.

A poem should be wordless,
Thus not exist.

A poem should be a thing
Which Horace wouldn't recognize.

A poem should never "mean"
(too bourgeoisie).

Carmen CI

Catullus
(Roman, 84–54 B.C.)

I've come across the nations and the seas,
beloved brother, to stand upon your grave,
to bring to you, at last, these gifts for the dead,
softly speaking, in vain, to your silent ashes.
The Fates have taken you away from me,
too soon, too premature, too unexpected.
Nevertheless, please accept these gifts,
in the tradition of our beloved forefathers,
as my tears rise again in my eyes and swell:
Goodbye, brother, forever. Hail and farewell!

To a Woman Passing By

Charles Baudelaire
(French, 1821–1867)

The deafening street was roaring all around me,
as a woman passed, in mourning, in majestic distress
and sorrow, so tall and slender. And I could see,
as she lifted with her hand, beneath the hem of her dress.
So graceful. I drank her in, as if insane:
the lovely legs, the eyes like the sky when it fills
with a forming tempest, a hurricane,
with a softness that fascinates, a pleasure that kills.
Like lightning, then darkness! Her beauty so sublime,
I felt reborn with a fleeting glance. But when
will I ever see her again? The end of time?
So distant! So far! Maybe even never again!
We don't even know where the other's going to,
O, woman, whom I could have loved. O, woman, who knew!

Portugal

Miguel de Unamuno
(Spanish, 1864–1936)

At the farthest edge of the Atlantic shore,
a barefoot and disheveled lady peers
into the waves, at the foot of the mountains, and hears
the distant, weeping pines. She sits before
the swirling sea, propping her head in her hands,
and like a lioness, fixes her gazing eyes
on the gateway of the sun, while the ocean cries
its tragic songs of wonders and distant lands.
It sings of tragedies and fate, while she,
with her feet in the foaming surf, dreams of history —
dreams of that once-great empire doomed to be,
so suddenly, lost and drowned in the gloomy sea —
then stares, through the mist, as the King of mystery,
Dom Sebastian, rises from the sea.

December

Fra. Cesare Angelini
(Italian, 1886–1973)

December, the month of that most holy day,
which makes Christian even the falling snow.
(In whisper, the winds tell everything they know
to the forest and the pebbles in the river-spray.)
And every soul, at this great story, awakens afresh,
reviving their childhoods from ages gone by.
(The country churches speak out and testify,
and all the earth is one great festive crèche.)
Is it snowing again in the countryside?
Where homes, in vigil, comfort and console,
where words, now full of depth, are intensified.
Jesus, tonight, will come again and stay
with the beggar, the finch, and the wandering soul,
who, like a leaf, flutters along the way.

Autopsychography

Fernando Pessoa
(Portuguese, 1888–1935)

The poet is a faker,
whose faking is so real,
he even fakes the pain
he actually can feel.

And those who read his poems
don't feel his pain but feel
a pain they really don't have,
that's not exactly real.

While whizzing around the track,
amusing our minds with art,
there circles the wind-up train
we call the human heart.

Portrait

Cecília Meireles
(Brazilian, 1901–1964)

I didn't always have the face I have today,
so calm, so sad, so thin,
nor these vacant eyes,
nor these bitter lips.

I didn't always have these useless hands,
so cold, so still, so dead,
nor did I have this heart
which never reveals itself.

Nor did I sense the changes when they came,
so simple, so certain, so easy:
In which mirror did I lose
my other face?

The Ballad of Jeanne Bertaut

After Maurois

At the death of Jeanne Bertaut,
at the age of thirty-one,
we all expected her husband's career
would soon be over and done.

When Victor Bertaut had married Jeanne
several years ago,
he was a dazzling orator,
and a bit of a Romeo.

He was also vain and rude and crude,
too ambitious for his age,
impossible to get along with,
and given to fits of rage.

But Jeanne soon saved him from himself,
being smart and thoughtful and kind,
she calmed him down and helped her lover
focus his brilliant mind.

So he went from being a political "crank"
to a bright star on the rise,
but, now, his guardian angel was buried
beneath the Parisian skies.

It didn't take long for his troubles to start,
each of his own design,
and when he insulted Cheron in the Chamber,
he felt it was time to resign.

Then Victor received an unusual letter,
a letter from the dead,
a letter from his loving wife,
and he read every word she said.

It seems that Jeanne foresaw his troubles,
on her deathbed near the end,
and gave a personal handwritten letter
to a secret trusted friend.

The very next day, Victor Bertaut
did exactly as advised;
standing before Cheron in the Chamber,
he humbly apologized.

But, in Morocco, a few months later,
enjoying a rare vacation,
he met the beautiful Dora Bergmann
and couldn't resist temptation.

Dora, a stunning adventuress,
was anything but shy,
a "poet-explorer" with a shady past,
and rumored to be a spy.

When Victor decided to propose to Dora,
having fallen under her spell,
a second letter from the dead
arrived at his hotel.

He read the letter, broke things off,
and returned to the River Seine,
while Dora retreated to Western Sahara
to explore the desert terrain.

Then, two years later, Bertaut met Aimé,
who was lovely as she could be,
but he was wary of committing himself,
fearing catastrophe.

When the final letter came,
he bought a diamond ring,
and they married happily-ever-after
in the warm Parisian spring.

But, often, he visits his guardian angel,
who taught him how to behave,
from her tomb in Père Lachaise
with letters from the grave.

The Abbé of the Avant-garde

At chic affairs that scintillate,
he makes his minions suspirate
with all his *très* vogue skepticism
and anti-papal pantheism.
An evolution Jacobin,
he scoffs at Adam and his sin,
then argues for his Indexed opus,
and his monkey, Sinanthropus.

Then, without the slightest shame,
he murmurs, "*Oui*, I've won the game!"
The faith is reeling on the rocks,
beside the père's Pandora's box.
But when the blackness comes, he gropes,
and cries out for his forfeit hopes,
then stumbles down the nether zones,
with old test tubes and monkey bones.

The Journalist of Reputation

Who cares about his active crotch,
the opium, the quarts of scotch,
compulsive lies (a small faux pas),
the Satan rites, ménage *à trois*,
deserted mistress, abandoned son,
and all the other bits of fun?
Let's give this prince of blackest lies
the *Times* front page, the Pulitzer Prize.

He'd seen the corpses in the street
rotting in the summer heat,
but what's a couple million dead?
it's best to leave the thing unsaid.
He had his girls, his perks, his booze,
and never put it in the news,
He liked the tyrant and his "ism,"
and "tough," "committed" journalism.

The Poet Moderne

Two fifths talent, three fifths fake,
out from the valley of the snake,
with earring, cape, and red-forked beard,
he sniffed around, and then he sneered:
it's time to toss the live grenade,
there's too much art that's retrograde,
and so he struck the Modern's pose,
and poetry became like prose.

But after all the fame and treason,
the arrogance, and smug unreason,
his thoughts grew much less doctrinaire
and crashed into a dark despair.
He called his work a "botch," "not art,"
lacking form, and lacking heart,
and cried out loud and cried it long:
"*Always*, *always*, I've been wrong!"

The Scientist of the Mind

Gnosticism, ESP,
cocaine, and numerology,
the paranormal, mesmerism,
lots of sex and atheism.
No wonder every male's elation
to comprehend about castration,
the lurid charms of the female bust,
and all such therapeutic lust.

But solid scientific query
negates his methods and his theory,
and now, it's clear he faked the facts,
he cited in his faddish tracts.
And now, sometimes, awake at night,
he tosses in the doubter's fright,
and hears his conscience whisper, "quack!"
and, sometimes, "megalomaniac!"

The Artist of Fashion

Up, then down, the boulevard,
he led the bloody avant-garde,
and shocked the bores who bought his "spit"
and reveled in the counterfeit.
And everything he did was news:
he'd hurt the girls and beat the muse,
then conjure from some "current" ditch,
and play the game till he got rich.

And each and every academian
fell before this chic bohemian.
Yes, Paris found him *hors concours*
and begged for more and more and more.
But now, late nights, when death comes near,
he thinks of Giotto and Vermeer,
of Titian, and the other greats,
and, in the dark, asphyxiates.

The Playwright of the People

He always wears his workers' grey,
even to the matinee,
and claims the masses "paramount"
yet keeps a silent Swiss account.
And always at his lake estate,
he makes the young girls fornicate,
then writes dull scenes of dark ennui
which castigate the bourgeoisie.

He loves the voids of cynicism
and every other vile "ism."
And when his masters crushed a "plot,"
he said the blameless should be shot.
"For life's a swindle and art's a cheat,
both clever frauds and low deceit."
And now he lies, just like his art,
a steel stiletto through his heart.

The Philosopher of Action

Unwashed, defiant, all the rage,
he calmly walks across the stage,
and rails against this dark abyss
where God's a dead hypothesis,
and curses down some vague élite
and calls for murder in the street.
But late that night, feeling no pain,
he sings jazz songs and drinks champagne.

But soon, he drinks till he's flat drunk
then falls into a frightening funk,
still loudly damning those who snigger
that he's the son of old Heidegger.
And when his ladies get him home,
in the dark, he shakes alone,
and sees the time, with dread dismay,
when all his books will be passé.

Visiting All the Places We Once Made Love

I'm visiting all the places we once made love,
thinking of what's been lost, thinking of you,
which everyone calls "pathetic" and "unheard of."
But I visit the places where we once made love:
the beach, the lake, the garden, the balcony above,
the baseball field, still wet with the morning dew.
I'm visiting all the places we once made love,
thinking of what's been lost, and missing you.

Agenda

What's the hidden agenda in my baby's heart?
The greatest secret ever unknown.
Which I'd like to know, but wouldn't know where to start.
What's the hidden agenda in my baby's heart?
But maybe "wanting to know" is not too smart;
surely it's best to leave unknowns alone.
What's the hidden agenda in my baby's heart?
The greatest mystery ever-forever unknown.

A Descent into the Maelström

Off the Norwegian coast

Downward toward the whirling pit,
from my schooner's deck I fell,
holding just the wooden cask,
headlong down the walls of hell.

Swirling centrifugal forces
slam me hard against the steep,
blackish, liquid walls of death,
more than forty fathoms deep.

Trapped within its awesome power,
thinking of my sons, I pray,
hopeless, yet, accepting fate,
ready, now, to die this way.

Whirling in the sickly chaos,
frenzied circuits, round and round,
both my brothers' cries are lost
in the whirlpool's shrieking sound.

Down below, our schooner plunges
to the rocky base of hell.
Who'd believe what I have seen,
should I somehow live to tell?

Transgression

It's now time for us both to remember
when the God-had-forbidden took place,
when we did what I did what you did
and the subsequent guilt and disgrace.

When you sat in the station beside me,
and you cried in the soft April rain,
when you finally decided to leave me,
and you kissed me and left on the train.

It's now time for us both to remember
when our love was indulgent and true
when we were fantastic young lovers,
and no one ever "got me" like you.

When our love was champagne and red roses,
and holding each other at night,
until what would happen had happened,
we embraced in a lovers' delight.

Now it's time for us both to forget
our youthful unspoken dark crime.
Now it's time for us both to remember
that our time will be soon out of time.

The Little Boy Who Couldn't Rhyme

There once was a little boy who couldn't rhyme,
not even for his sister. Not anytime.

Maybe it was because he was so sad;
nothing seemed to make him *truly* glad.

He'd walk, and talk, and eat at suppertime,
but he couldn't smile, and he couldn't rhyme.

Even when his sister would rhyme a tune
about a hammer and a fat balloon.

He couldn't rhyme "balloon" with "rocky raccoon,"
or "Saskatoon" or "Daniel Boone."

He tried, of course, with his sister and his dad,
but rhymes come from the heart, and he was too sad.

Once their house was full of rhymes and songs,
poems, and Mother Goose, and sing-alongs.

But that was before his mother went away.
To heaven. And now he missed her every day.

He missed her voice, her smile, her happy rhymes,
and what she'd told them so many, many times:

“Rhyming’s like making sweets for your sisters and brothers:
You don’t do it just for yourself; you do it for others!”

Then every night, she’d say, “Hug me good-night,”
and he’d say, “All right, but tight!” and she’d laugh, “Quite right!”

But now when his sister played the rhyming game,
he couldn’t. Or wouldn’t. It just wasn’t the same.

Then his sister would say, without getting mad,
“Mommy doesn’t want us to be so sad.”

“Besides,” she’d say, “I *couldn’t* live without rhyme!
It’s like toys, and candy, and love, and Christmas time!”

One night, he dreamed his mother came with a rhyme:
“You’ll chime, my dear, a rhyme whenever it’s time.”

One day, when his sister had baked a cake,
they took a walk in the woods near a frozen lake.

It was very cold and snowy, but wintry nice,
until she slipped and crashed down on the ice.

She didn’t move. He feared she might be dead.
So he got his father, who carried her up to bed.

But when she didn’t wake, they carried her down
and drove her over to the clinic in town.

Where all the doctors looked worried and sad,
explaining words like “coma” to his dad.

So they sat together at her hospital bed all night,
as father prayed, and whispered, "It'll be all right."

But the little boy wasn't so sure that it was true,
and he wished that there was something he could do.

Later, when his dad fell asleep in a chair,
the boy stood next to her bed, touching her hair.

He thought he heard her mumble, one more time,
so softly: "I *couldn't* live without rhyme."

"Well, then," he said, "let's try a few:
like 'cockatoo,' 'boo-hoo,' and 'Kathmandu.'"

When she smiled, though her eyes were still shut tight,
he whispered, "'dynamite' and 'fahrenheit.'"

And he kept rhyming rhymes all night long;
some he whispered, others he'd sing in song.

Sometimes she'd smile, and sometimes he would too,
at "peek-a-boo," and "true," and "I love you."

And when his dad woke up, he joined right in,
with "violin," and "gin," and "rolling pin."

Until she opened her eyes and said,
"gingerbread," "red," and "go-ahead!"

They laughed, and holding hands with each other,
she whispered, "Thank you, my dear little brother."

"Yes!" their dad agreed, "What a wonderful day!
Let's remember what mommy used to say:

"'Rhyming's like making sweets for your sisters and brothers:
You don't do it just for yourself; you do it for others!'"

So now there's a little boy who loves to rhyme,
with his sister, with his dad, or anytime!

Prince Charming

For Maggie and Billy

When the path of Prince Charming gets bumpy,
he never complains or gets *grumpy*:
not even when he trips on a rock,
or gets duped by a trollish old *doc*,
not even when sick, feeling queasy,
coughy, and wheezy, and *sneezy*,
not even when witches get creepy,
casting spells and making him *sleepy*,
not even when his horse gets mopey,
or he's feeling tired and *dopey*,
'cause he'll hum a love song from Nashville,
think of Snow White, and get *bashful*,
then he'll find her and kiss her right snappy,
and they'll marry at once and be *happy*!

Little Willie

Little Willie, dueling one day,
stabbed his dad in the eye, "Touché!"
Mother looked over, approved, "Well done!
Cause all he really needs is one."

Little Willie got out of bed
and shot a hole through Daddy's head;
Mother, shocked, looked over, "Great Scott!
My dearest boy, what an excellent shot!"

Little Willie broke Suzie's heart,
À la mode, à la carte;
Mother approved, "She's such a bore!
Good boy, Willie, break some more!"

Caesar

Jorge Luis Borges
(Argentine, 1889–1986)

Here's what the daggers have left on the ground,
this poor pathetic thing, a man who's bled
to death, whose name was "Caesar." The blades have found
their mark, slashing the flesh of the one-now-dead.
So here he lies, after their atrocious crime,
a dead machine used, yesterday, to live
for fame, to execute the history of his time,
enjoying everything his life could give.
But here's *another*, an emperor so discrete
and prudent that once he felt it best
to decline the crown, while commanding the Roman fleet
and the army which conquered both East and West.
Here's, also, *another* — the one to come — who's hurled
his awesome shadow across the world.

On His Blindness

Jorge Luis Borges
(Argentine, 1889–1986)

To the end of my years, I'm wrapped in a shining mist,
a stubborn haze that always hovers near
and reduces all things down to one: to co-exist
without color or form. Almost, to an idea.
The vast elemental night and day,
so full of people, seem nothing but a haze
of light, uncertain yet true, which never fades away,
and lurks in every dawn. I wish I could gaze
upon a face sometime. Or appreciate
these encyclopedias, or other books I hold
in my hands but never can read, or the great
high-soaring birds, or the moons of gold.
For others, there remains the universe,
but in my penumbra, only the habits of verse.

A Morning in 1649

Jorge Luis Borges
(Argentine, 1889–1986)

Charles advances among his people and glances
right and left. Alone, dismissing his well-bred
palace attendants, he calmly walks ahead,
free from self-deception, accepting his circumstances.
He knows he's the king. He knows, not far from here,
he goes to death, though not, he also knows,
into oblivion. The terrible morning grows
more real, his execution waits, but he has no fear.
Like a good gambler, he's always been somewhat
aloof, living his life to the full. Unbowed,
he moves throughout the dangerous crowd.
The chopping block brings no disgrace. His judges are *not*
the ultimate Judge. And then, despite his present trials,
he nods, as he's done so often before, and smiles.

A Poet of the 13th Century

Jorge Luis Borges
(Argentine, 1889–1986)

Once again, he studies the laborious draft
of the very first sonnet, as yet unnamed:
still arbitrary, with its poorly-framed
quatrains and tercets, still lacking the formal craft.
Revising, slowly, he suddenly prevails.
He stops. Something flashes from a future time,
something wondrous, frightening, even sublime,
like the melodious murmur of distant nightingales.
Does he realize that many more sonnets will follow?
That mysterious, incredible Apollo
has revealed a secret, an archetypal thing,
which like a greedy crystal attracts then steals
all that the night conceals and the day reveals:
Daedalus, the maze, the riddle, and Oedipus the King?

A Soldier of Urbina

Jorge Luis Borges
(Argentine, 1889–1986)

(Cervantes)

Feeling unworthy of yet another campaign,
like his last battle bravely fought at sea,
the soldier, wanders alone in obscurity,
resigned to sordid jobs throughout his native Spain.
To erase, or mitigate, the blackened night
of his reality, he hides within a vast
domain of dreams, within a magical past,
within the cycles of Roland, the Breton knight.
Yet, still, he contemplates his deepest pain,
at sunset, observing the copper-colored plain,
convinced he's finished: lonely, impoverished, unknown.
Unaware of the special music which he alone
possesses, where Quixote and Panza and all their schemes
are already stirring alive at the depths of his dreams.

Texas

Jorge Luis Borges
(Argentine, 1889–1986)

Here too. Here, at the edge of another sea
and continent, there lies another new
and boundless plain where voices vanish and die. Here too:
the Indian, the lasso, and horses running free.
Here too: that secret bird whose sweet song glides
above the roar of historical time, reviving anew
the memory of a forgotten afternoon. Here too:
that mystic alphabet of stars which guides
my pen to scrawl these names from long ago,
still undisturbed within the endless flow
of the labyrinth of time: San Jacinto,
and that second Thermopylae, the Alamo.
Here too: that strange, incomprehensible strife,
so brief, so anxious, that we know as life.

To an Old Poet

Jorge Luis Borges
(Argentine, 1889–1986)

(Quevedo)

In the country fields of Castile, you walk about,
self-absorbed, aware of nothing and no one.
You reflect on some intricate verse from John, without
a single glance at the yellow, setting sun.
But the shifting, dying light, like a ranting fool,
grows delirious, and high above your path
in the east, there expands the scarlet moon of ridicule
and mockery, which just might be the "Mirror of Wrath."
You raise your eyes and stare into the skies,
and a memory of something, something remote,
begins to form but then extinguishes and dies.
Sadly, with your head hung low, you'll soon
continue on your way, having forgotten what you wrote
years ago: *His epitaph is a bloody moon.*

The History of Western Poetry

Meter, of course, is classicist;
Rhyme is Catholic-medieval;.
Blank verse is lapsed and Anglicist;
Vers libre is French (and evil).

II. *The Unfortunates* (1997)

Breaking and Entering

When he was done, he sat in their living room:
as always, he'd made certain they'd be away,
and checked for dogs, alarms, and nosy neighbors,
then glass-cut through a window in the back,
ready with the knife he'd never used
(but would), and quickly packed her gold and stones,
their small antiques, the "knock-out" Tiffany lamp,
which these dull bastards certainly didn't deserve.

But he liked their quiet house, just like he'd liked
his parents' best when they were sound asleep,
no nagging, fighting, or banging him about.
Some "sneaks" enjoy the breaking in — "like sex,"
they say — while others crave the risks, or just the goods,
but he liked sitting in their living rooms,
until, at last, he'd slit their couches open and leave.
Too bad. He liked it here; it felt like home.

Hospital

A noise. She wakes alone into the dark,
and feels the anesthetic in her veins
and all the catheters, and IV lines,
and other things still keeping her alive.
Unable to move, she watches the monitor lights,
strange blues and reds, of countless medical machines.
Her operation's done, and now she cries,
maybe, one might think, from pain or fear.

But she recalls that summer in her youth,
and how they raced across a lovers' Europe,
and how they loved, especially in Spain,
until that little quarrel in Barcelona,
and how she woke alone the very next day,
and he was gone, for good, forever,
but she'd refused to cry. Until right now.
One might survive disease, but never that.

Prosecutor

Another homicide, another trial.
He hated every single bit of it.
So why did he still bother? He seldom saw
his wife these days; his paycheck was a joke;
and the boss was nothing but a petty party hack
scheming to be governor. It also
wasn't the murder scenes, the sleazy lawyers,
soft judges, lying witnesses, and timid juries.

It also wasn't some personal vendetta
against the thugs, the whores, the psychopaths.
Even noble notions about "justice"
weren't enough anymore. But still, he knew why,
watching the trembling, devastated father
of the dead Hispanic girl
— battered, raped, stabbed over 25 times —
unable to hold his shaking cup of coffee.

Librarian

Once she liked to log and stack the books
in order — neat and perfect — all those marvelous books
so full of wisdom, both comprehensible
and far beyond her grasp. She'd disciplined herself
to tolerate the patrons, but things had gotten worse.
The "dolt" percent had risen fast: "Where's
the latest diet book?" or "Nostradamus?"
or "water sports?" Not exactly Milton or Plato.

But she, herself, had also changed, especially since
she'd dumped her Jack for Steve then lost them both.
Lately, even the books were getting on her nerves.
So she began to sneak the classics home
at night — no one seemed to notice —
and buy the garden hoses, because tonight
she planned to soak this place into a swamp
of swollen, damp, disgusting books.

Trauma Center

They flew him in by chopper late last night:
the slug, a .38, had missed his heart,
but left a bloody, mangled mess inside.
More than once, he'd saved this punk before,
the eldest of the infamous Davis brothers,
a violent pimp and pusher who'd told him once,
"I'm indestructible, man," and then, another
time, "I've put six suckers in the box."

At 6:00 a.m., the apprehensive surgeon
rechecked the room, which was, as he expected,
empty. Once again, the man had yanked
away his IV lines and risen up,
with the hole right through his chest, and slithered back
into the Newark streets, looking for "action,"
drugs, and prey — amid your sons and daughters —
exactly where his surgeon's knife had put him.

Garbage

She sorted though it very carefully:
the coffee grounds, the high-fat foods, the filters
of his cigarettes — *He's smoking again!* —
a new rosé, her favorite shaving cream —
she smelled the empty can — the same junk mail
he'd gotten for years. Until the restraining order,
she used to follow him everywhere he went,
then, for a while, she stole his mail.

Her useless friends discarded her as well:
"Modern women don't behave like that."
Well, maybe not. She pushed aside some canceled
checks. What's this? A woman's business card.
Maybe that slinky blonde from Queens? She flipped it over:
"Stay the hell away from my garbage, you sicko!"
She jolted back, in shock and fear: *He knows!*
Now she couldn't even trust his garbage.

Confidence Man

Casually, he glanced across the courtroom,
checking out the twelve dimwitted jurors.
The foxy chick in the designer clothes
reminded him of an early mark, years ago,
in Baltimore, his second Pigeon Drop.
Those were the days, with all the classic bunco:
Jamaican Hustles, the Indian Penny Scam,
the Violin, the Diamond Ring, and the Missing Heir.

While other kids went off to loaf at college,
he played the sucker scams, respecting only
those who didn't take the bait up-front,
and he had other standards too: no charity fraud,
no elderly marks, no disaster victims.
He also never used his charm and "knock-out" looks
for quickie sex with eager female dupes.
Business was business, and sex was a different scam.

He glanced at both his "victims" (plaintiffs),
Mr. Jerk and Mrs. Bitch, and managed
not to smile. He'd sold the greedy bastards
600 acres of prime Nevada wasteland,
for "oil leasing," at 500 bucks an acre —
which cost him 3 apiece — where the only oil,
for 200 miles, was lubing through the tourist
vans that cruised down Highway 41.

He'd met them at the Pineview Country Club
on a Friday night and closed the deal on Monday,
and *that* was the "kick," the personal payoff:
not the money, but watching their pathetic greed
expand to something inexhaustibly grotesque,
until the "blow off" finally came, leaving
them devastated, humiliated, and crushed,
exactly as they both deserved to be.

And now, the Feds had brought him back in chains,
from Honolulu, after the fluke arrest —
Mrs. Bitch's vacationing sister had seen him
dining at the elegant Kulu in Waikiki —
and yet, despite what everyone might think,
he was enjoying himself. Sure he was clever,
and handsome, and quite an actor, but he was also
the foremost master of the "paperless" trail.

They'd never even know about the "super" stuff:
the shelter frauds, computer scams, and precious
metal rip-offs — or the millions in Zurich,
the condos, or the Mediterranean villas.
They'd also never know that he *loved* this "house of cards,"
the U.S. courts — the biggest scam of all —
where nothing counts but brass, deception, and fraud,
some things he knew a little bit about.

An "expert" shrink, another kind of con,
was talking in the witness box
about his manic and depressive states,
wild delusions, personality splits,
and his abusive, dysfunctional parents.

Again, he kept from smiling, even laughing;
he'd *never* been depressed in his whole life,
and his mom and dad — rest in peace — were perfect saints.

"Mr. Wesley might appear contrite,"
the D.A. later said in his summation,
"but he's a ruthless wrecker of peoples' lives."
Remorsefully, "Wesley" looked around —
these morons didn't even know his name,
or the sixteen other false identities,
or the wife (with kids) in Jersey, or the one
in Vegas, or the latest one on Maui.

Sentence: two months suspended, three community service,
repay the money, cover their legal fees,
and suffer through the lecture by the judge. Not bad.
He *loved* this country — the land of marks and suckers,
with all its mushy laws, and covetousness,
its freedom to do most any damned thing
under the sun, and its judiciary con,
where one, with certain skills, could scam the scam.

Runway

Was it really her he saw last night?
Sitting in a limousine at 67th
Street near Tavern on the Green?
Expressionless, yet just as beautiful
as twenty years ago, when he'd pursued her
at the Jersey shore. Until one night
she said, "All right," and took him to the airport
at two a.m. and climbed beneath the fence.

Then, side by side, they lay down in a ditch
in front of Runway 12. She held him close,
and then he saw it, huge, with flashing lights,
descending from the sky, like a bird of prey,
tremendous, closer, falling down upon them,
then roaring over their heads onto the runway —
and she looked into his eyes, as if to say,
"*This* is what life with me is like!"

East River

He sat at the Brooklyn end of the bridge
and stared below into the dark East River.
Forty years ago, his father tried to jump,
not even sure if it would take his life.
His fiancée had left him only a note
— full of strange, incomprehensible darkness —
then sailed back home, alone, to Bučovice
where life was hard, but, nevertheless, was home.

And now, tonight, his father was dead;
the cancer like a black and flowing river.
He lifted his eyes up to the blazing city:
"It gives you what you're worth," his father would say,
of the city he loved, when life, even here, was hard.
And then, from across the river, he heard the siren,
an ambulance racing through the city nights
taking away the ones we love.

Telephone Psychic

"He'll be very kind and thoughtful and he'll *love*
the movies!" Picking up her envelope,
she glanced across her long red nails, "You'll meet
him in the next few months." She truly *loved*
this job, always using her imagination.
She took her paycheck out and winked at Connie
in the corner cubicle. As long as "Jane" believes
that something will happen, then, probably, it will.

Oh, sure, it's all a "lie" — as mom so bluntly
puts it — yet it's just a kind of "whitish" lie:
putting her clients in a healthy frame of mind.
Like when her dad would call to tell her that
his tests were negative; or when her son
would reassure her that he'd given up the drugs;
or when, tonight, her husband called from Al's
Blue Star Motel to say he's working late.

Monte Carlo

The chic American girl, unescorted,
waits in the elegant *salon privé.*
The house has cleared the bet. Two million francs.
She puts it on "*noir*" and watches the wheel,
as everyone watches *her*. "The betting is closed."
Despite Pascal, despite the theory of large numbers,
she's known to be a careful "system" player:
decisive, sure, and confident. Yet, not really:

If "red," she loses everything she has;
she'll have to meet the count in Saint-Tropez.
If "black," she wins; she'll take her handsome Greek
to Paros for the month of June.
With little interest, she watches the wheel. "*Zero*!"
One in thirty-seven. The house wins. She leaves —
to do what she has always done on zero:
go back home and see her mom in Maine.

Disphobic

It's somewhat comforting to live one's life
with known, identifiable, phobic problems.
Like Jeanne, who hasn't flown a plane in years
because the very thought will palpitate
her heart until she hyperventilates,
with cold adrenaline gushing through her veins,
with nausea and debilitating freezing sweats,
until she wishes she were dead.

Like Anthony, who panics in the dark,
or Jack, who dreads the smell and look of fire,
or Mary Ann, who never leaves her house.
But what's it called when someone has the dark
and terrifying fear that all his sins
relentlessly, are stalking in the night,
all the more brazen for not having
a recognizable, scientific name?

Suicide Note

The night that she committed suicide:
her brother in New Jersey played the horses,
drinking with his buddies all night long;
her friend at Yale thumbed through a recent novel
looking in vain for meaning and for love;
her mother was asleep in New Rochelle;
her father, dead, was knocking on his box,
hoping to distract his little girl.

Her former lover, somewhere at the Cape,
was lying with a pretty undergrad,
content to think of anything but her.
Then someone read the poem beside her body,
which completely ignored the darkness in her mind,
and why her suicidal note was blank,
as everyone hurtled through the dark of space
sitting on their little, moist, blue rock.

III. *"Borges" and Other Sonnets* (2003)

Quarantine

If she lived across the city, he'd be out the door,
racing through the streets at the speed of light;
if she lived across the country, he'd jet from shore
to shore, as fast as he could, arriving tonight.
If she lived across the world, he'd track her down,
no matter how, to throw himself at her feet.
But she's sits across the room in her sleeping gown,
reading, and looking so lovely, remote, discreet,
across a cold, unpassable, infinite distance,
pulverizing his love with her bizarre
frigidity, her soulless non-existence,
and, yet, he'll stay with his love, so near, so far,
who's cut off everyone else, as well,
needing nothing but him in her companionless hell.

Firebrand

Beware. My genesis is now. I rise,
miraculously, from the black abyss,
I breathe, I swelter, and I oxidize
into a frenzy of pyrolysis.
A speck of flameless fire, I multiply,
foreseeing, even guaranteeing,
the burn and scorch of all this earth and sky,
and best of all, the flesh of the human being.
And when I'm done, when all the seas are dry,
the bluish planet will float through the smothering night
as black and vapid in the skyless sky
as its pathetic ugly satellite.
Like sin, deceit, and lust, I'm everywhere,
scheming your incineration. Beware.

Lecture

The hip professor lectured to his class,
this afternoon, but not a sound was heard,
which looked quite odd, and certainly didn't pass
unnoticed, but no one said a word.
Why bother? His students had better things to think
about: their dreams, their loves, their wedding rings,
and where they'd eat tonight, and what they'd drink,
and death, and cancer, and serious family things.
He finished. Class dismissed. It was, he thought,
his best performance of the year. A notion
his students supported, having never bought
his clever cynicism and self-promotion,
thinking it's better to learn nothing today
than learn whatever crap he couldn't say.

The Scream

Gathering firewood, startled by the sound,
he glances down at the lake, endless with snow
and little else but death, for miles around
in the crushing cold. It's nearly ten below.
She'll arrive tomorrow morning, just
as planned, undressing, as she (and he) embrace
the solitude of their weekend of lust
and daiquiris in front of the fireplace.
Up on the porch, he hears the cry again,
shivering in the cold; he won't admit
how human it sounds, or how familiar, and then
he makes up his mind, thinking, "The hell with it,"
forgetting whatever he's heard, even before
he steps inside, and firmly locks the door.

Secret Police

They're listening: at home (asleep/awake),
on the phone, at work, in the car, everywhere,
writing it down, hoping for some mistake,
knowing full well, I'm sure, that I *know* they're there.
So I read, out loud, my poems about her face,
her touch, her lips, and how she sets me free
— her sensuous caress, her loving embrace —
and I make those bastards wish that they were me.
Of course, not a single word of it is true,
but it's all that I've got. I'll *never* succumb
to those evil creeps: I'll hurt them back, and screw
their hearts, deep in the voids that they've become.
Two can play this game. Never presume
too much. After all, who's doing what to whom?

Pumpkin

This one's different. Yes, there's the flickering grins,
the hollow head, the candle-brain that glows
within, but this one somehow "knows" her sins,
her darkest secrets, knowing what no one knows:
exactly what she did that rainy night
when she was seventeen; the honeymoon
deceits; the letters she burned in the firelight;
the rendezvous at Westwood Lake last June.
It even knows that soon, she'll march, incensed,
across the room, and grab its head, and spin
around, and smash its leering face against
the kitchen floor, just as the kids come in,
stunned and wondering, "What's wrong with Mom?"
who stands in her orange mess like a ticking bomb.

Rattler

Madder than hell, it shoots up in the black,
fanged, its rattle shrilling catastrophe,
ready to strike, a venomed Diamondback,
warning, with death-blank eyes: "Don't mess with me."
The stranger stops and stares. He isn't surprised.
He knows these rattlers well. They can survive
most anything. Once, they'd terrorized
the West, killing more than the Colt .45.
But he's dead calm, eerily serene,
then whispers, as he'd done, with more at stake,
three years ago when he turned seventeen,
eyeing his father, another kind of snake,
just as venomous and serpentine:
"You go your way, and I'll go mine."

Footnote

* I lied. [When he left and said he didn't love
you anymore, that he needed to find
some space to grow as a person, above
all, as an artist, a writer of some kind,
living his 32 more years, thinking,
every single day (every one),
about your face, your touch, and the foul, stinking
unredeemably-stupid thing he'd done,
dying alone, aware that he'd become
a writer of no consequence, who'd been
a hack, and even worse, who'd never come
within a country mile of love again,
whose life was less than a silly anecdote:
an empty cipher and a two-word note.]

The Poem

When did the little poem get suicidal?
Maybe in revision, all those times
the syntax failed. Maybe lying idle,
stuck at thirteen lines with lousy rhymes.
First, you start to doubt yourself, to feel
incapable, and hopelessly unable
to succeed, feeling oddly unreal,
and bitter, edgy, erratic, and unstable.
Then depression sets in: despair, self-hate,
assuming, like all other self-abusers,
the worst, expecting that unspeakable fate
of all would-be sonnets and other losers:
to someday, suddenly, just disappear
into the trash, your throat slit ear to ear.

Balcony

“Please, just listen, and please don’t turn around.
Keep staring at the sea. It’s a marvelous view
tonight; the waves are beautiful, profound,
and so seductively close, just like you.
I love you. There, I’ve said it. I’ve seen it in
your eyes as well. Forgive me. I can’t restrain
myself. Maybe it’s seeing you move within
that dress, under the stars, sipping champagne.
And yet, we can’t be lovers. Not now. Not ever.
So if you love me, stay here in the evening light
and never say a word.” She didn’t. Never.
He left, and didn’t sleep at all that night,
watching his wife, thinking, although he knew,
it was inadequate, “I love you, too.”

The Odyssey, Book Twenty-Three

Jorge Luis Borges
(Argentine, 1889–1986)

Already the iron sword of the king has spread
its bloody vengeance. Justice is done.
His arrows and lance have found each and every one
of the insolent suitors who now lie bloodless and dead.
Despite the efforts of a god to undermine
this king, Ulysses has returned to queen and realm,
in spite of storming plots to overwhelm
his ship, in spite of Ares' cries and murderous design.
And now, in the warm love of their bridal bed,
the luminous queen lies sleeping with her head
on the chest of her king. So where's that castaway
who during his exile, night and day, would run
across the world like a wild dog and say
to monsters that his name was "No One"?

The Borges

Jorge Luis Borges
(Argentine, 1889–1986)

I know little or nothing of the Borges,
my ancestors, those Portuguese people lurking here
within my flesh, whose obscure but permanent trace
remains: their habits, their rigor, and their fear.
Shadowy, as if they'd never seen the sun,
these strangers to the processes of art
still form, indecipherably, a part
of time, of earth, and of oblivion.
And justly so, because their labors have prevailed:
they're Portugal — that famous race, at whose command,
the Great Walls of the East were breached, who sailed
out across the seas, to other seas of sand.
They are that fearless king who vanished inside
the desert, and those, back home, who swear he never died.

To Luís de Camões

Jorge Luis Borges
(Argentine, 1889–1986)

Without a shred of pity, time dulls the most
heroic swords, and now, sad Captain, your command
is done, and you've come home to the nostalgic coast
to die within, and with, your native land.
On distant, enchanted, foreign deserts, the flower
of Portugal was lost, unable to endure;
while Spain, no longer subdued and flush with power,
threatens your borders and unprotected shore.
I wonder if you ever understood,
before you crossed that final shore to final rest,
that *everything* which seemed lost and gone for good
— your sword, your flag, the Orient, and the West —
would resurrect, free from the human curse
of change, in *Os Lusíadas*, your epic verse.

The Sea

Jorge Luis Borges
(Argentine, 1889–1986)

Before our dreams (or terrors) persisted
in mythology and cosmogony,
even before time coined itself in days, there existed,
already, the sea. It *was*. There was *always* the sea.
But *who* is the sea? Who is that old, undisciplined,
violent creature, who's gnawing away under
the pillars of the earth, who's also chance and wind,
one and many oceans, abyss and wonder?
Staring upon the sea, we see it as though
for the first time, sensing the splendor of all free
and elemental things: like afternoons, the glow
of the moon, or a blazing fire. But who is the sea?
And who am I? In time, when my days are passed,
and my final agony's done, I'll know, at last.

Allusion to the Death of Colonel Francisco Borges (1835–1874)

Jorge Luis Borges
(Argentine, 1889–1986)

At dusk, I leave him riding on his horse
looking for death. Of all the hours of his past,
this is the image that I'd like to last,
with both its triumph and its bitter remorse.
Solemnly, he moves across the terrain
his white horse and poncho approaching his fate,
while Death, patient in the rifles, lies in wait.
Sadly, Francisco Borges crosses the plain.
This is what surrounds him now: the rifles' roar;
this is what he sees: the endless plains.
This has been his life, it's what remains,
and this has been his place: in battles and war.
So high on his horse in his epic universe,
I leave him as he is, untouched, almost, by my verse.

Snowflake

Timing's everything. The vapor rises
high in the sky, tossing to and fro,
then freezes, suddenly, and crystallizes
into a perfect flake of miraculous snow.
For countless miles, drifting east above
the world, whirling about in a swirling free-
for-all, appearing aimless, just like love,
but sensing, seeking-out, its destiny.
Falling to where the two young skaters stand,
hand in hand, then flips and dips and whips
itself about to ever-so-gently land,
a miracle, across her unkissed lips:
as he blocks the wind raging from the south,
leaning forward to kiss her lovely mouth.

Thief

He came one night last week. Taking his time,
he read my personal letters, used the phone,
and played the piano. Enjoying his casual crime,
he contaminated everything I own.
Two bored policemen came, "You have no proof
that anyone was here?" Careful, polite,
they took some useless notes, keeping aloof,
saying as they left, "So, nothing was taken, right?"
who never fathomed what had happened here:
how this supercilious creep had waded deep
into my life, and found nothing, it's clear,
that he might condescend to bother to keep.
He is, of course, the subtlest of thieves,
taking one's self-respect before he leaves.

Monster

It slithered down the funeral parlor halls,
coming like a plague, a death, a pox
on all their houses, sliming across the walls
above the silent dead-thing in her box.
It stared, then laughed grotesquely, unconcerned
and self-absorbed, but when her oh-so-grim
companion entered the room, the monster turned,
sensing an urge to rip him limb from limb,
but decided not to bother. No, instead,
it craved the dark, and left, skulking as far
away as it could get from the newly-dead.
Outside, it quickly scurried towards my car,
then somehow got inside and turned the key,
staring in the mirror, looking at me.

Confession

You've wanted to tell someone all day long:
exactly what you did back then, the scar
that festers, the unforgivable wrong.
Someone needs to know who you *really* are.
So you try to tell your friend at morning break;
then start to tell your mom at lunch, but stop,
you'd like everyone to know your filthy mistake,
at the bakery, the gym, and the coffee shop.
At home, you try to call it down to the street,
to expose your sinful self in the soft moonlight.
Then naked, ashamed, revolted by your life of deceit,
you lie in your bed and tell it to the night:
which hurts, no doubt, but still you call your bluff,
knowing that self-disgust is *never* enough.

Swimming Pool

Just one of those unexpected things in life:
he's heading behind the house after school
and sees her standing there, someone's wife,
undressing over the edge of her swimming pool.
Barefoot, she drops her robe to the ground. Within
the sultry-dark and muggy heats of the night,
her loveliness, her soft damp touchable skin,
luxurious, glows in the moon's faint light.
She swims a bit, then sits at the end of her day,
thinking of what? her past? a favorite song?
her husband? Silently rising, she walks away
and into her home. He waits, but not for long,
then enters the house; the air is fresh and cool;
his wife is waiting, still damp with the wet of the pool.

Conspiracy

You know the truth about the suicide
of the emissary's wife, the cocaine bust
in Venice, and the plagues at Passiontide.
But whom can you tell? Whom can you really trust?
Desperate, you fly to Washington, D.C.,
to your ex-lover. "Meet me anywhere."
"Of course," she says. "Let's meet at the N.S.C."
Later, walking from McPherson Square,
you start to tell her on the Mall, but "No,"
she puts a finger to your lips, "Don't say
a word. Please. I really don't want to know."
Instead, she kisses your mouth; you pull away.
You check your watch. It's two a.m.
There's not much time. Your love is one of *them*.

Last Will

And testament: Burn the books. Burn
the stupid manuscripts. Reconstitute
all assets into ready cash and turn
it over to the poor and destitute.
In the hope that I might somehow be forgiven
for what I've done, for my insensate pride,
for abandoning the gift (her) I was given,
using her, then shoving her aside.
In the hope that she has long forgotten me,
that she's been able, these thirty-two years, to fill
her life with happiness, that she's been free
from angst and its necrosis of the will.
In the hope that none of you (yes, *you*) will ever
screw-up your lives, losing your lover forever.

Labyrinth

The first year that I spent in hell
I staggered around the endless passageways,
blaspheming God, myself, and my prison cell:
this maddening, silent, and lonely maze.
The second year things changed. I looked around.
I thought of escape. I took some measurements,
made maps, concocted hypotheses, and found,
that even though all was hopeless, I was content.
The third year came, and I prayed with gratitude,
each day, for my little speck of infinity,
asking, only, for relief from my solitude.
Finally, a man approaches from Passage D:
He shakes my hand. He's proper and precise.
"I'm Señor Borges, welcome to Paradise."

IV. *Luís de Camões: Selected Sonnets* (2005)

Curse

Luís de Camões
(Portuguese, 1524–1580)

Wipe away, with death, the day of my birth;
may it be forgotten forever, and never
come back in the sweep of time. And if it ever
returns, eclipse the sun and blacken the earth.
Let all light fade and disappear. Let wild
omens reveal that everything must die.
Let monsters be born. Let blood rain from the sky.
Let every mother not recognize her child.
Let all the stunned and terrified people, with tears
streaking down their faces, pale and worn,
believe their world is doomed and overthrown.
You, frightened people, accept these wonders and fears,
for this was the wretched day on which was born
the most miserable life that ever was known.

Shipwreck

Luís de Camões
(Portuguese, 1524–1580)

Like a weary sailor, a refugee
from wreck and storm, who escapes half-dead,
and then, in terror, shudders with dread
at the very mention of the name of the "sea";
who swears he'll never sail again, who raves
he'll stay at home, even on the calmest days,
but then, in time, forgets his fearful ways,
and seeks, again, his fortune above the waves;
I, too, have barely escaped the storms that revolve
around you, my love, traveling far away,
vowing to avoid another catastrophe,
but I can't, the thought of you breaks my resolve,
and so, I return to where, on that fateful day,
I nearly drowned in your tempestuous sea.

Dear Gentle Soul

Luís de Camões
(Portuguese, 1524–1580)

Dear gentle soul, who has, too soon, departed
this life, so discontent: please rest, my dear,
forever in heaven, while I, remaining here,
must live alone, in pain, and broken-hearted.
Within your ethereal state, so high above,
if you are allowed to recall your life below,
remember what you saw, not long ago,
within my eyes, my perfect ardent love.
And if my pain has earned me some relief,
some dispensation, I wonder if you might
in prayer, ask God, who took away your brief
young life, if He would soon, this very night,
give me death, and end my helpless grief,
as swiftly as he took you from my sight.

Tagus

Luís de Camões
(Portuguese, 1524–1580)

Gentle waters of the Tagus, you flow
across the fields, nourishing the herds,
the blooming plants, the flowers, and the birds,
delighting the nymphs and shepherds as you go.
Sweet waters of the Tagus, I don't know when
I'll ever be able to come back home to you,
and, anxiously, before I say adieu,
I begin to doubt if I'll ever return again.
Destiny, intent on finding a way
to turn my joys to sorrows, now commands
this difficult parting, full of regrets and fears.
Still longing for you, and complaining, I sail away,
to breathe my sighs in the airs of foreign lands,
disturbing distant waters with my tears.

Natércia

Luís de Camões
(Portuguese, 1524–1580)

The flaming sun rises high, to the peak
of its ascent in the sky. The goat herds shrink
away from their sweltering fields to drink
the cool refreshing waters from the creek.
The birds, burning in the scorching glare,
find shelter beneath the leaves, within the shade,
and, yet, their lovely songs begin to fade,
and only the humming cicadas fill the air.
Liso is searching for his nymph, although
he always fails, no matter how he tries,
and with a thousand sighs, bemoans his lot.
"Why have you left the one who loves you so,
for one who loves you not?" young Liso cries,
and Echo answers softly, " . . . loves you not."

Escape

Luís de Camões
(Portuguese, 1524–1580)

How strange is life that she should choose to shun
the world, to run away from its deceit,
to hide her youth and beauty, and to retreat
beneath the cloak of a Franciscan nun!
But nothing can conceal her grace, mystique,
and marvelous eyes, nothing on earth can hide
her beauty which leaves me totally mystified,
without resistance, helpless and weak.
Whoever keeps her image in mind,
will never be free from pain and all these misguided
hopes and desires which Reason condemns. Whoever,
like me, has seen this glorious woman will find
himself enslaved, for Love has already decided
that she has conquered my heart forever.

Exile

Luís de Camões
(Portuguese, 1524–1580)

Here in this Babylon, that's festering
forth enough evil for the rest of the earth;
Here where true love is denied its worth,
where lustful Venus pollutes everything.
Here where evil is refined and good is cursed,
and tyranny, not honor, has its way;
Here where the Monarchy, in disarray,
blindly attempts to mislead God, and worse.
Here in this labyrinth, where Royalty,
willingly, chooses to succumb
before the Gates of Greed and Infamy;
Here in this murky chaos and delirium,
I carry out my tragic destiny.
But *never* will I forget you, Jerusalem!

Sin

Luís de Camões
(Portuguese, 1524–1580)

Happy is he whose only problem worth
complaining about is love's audacious schemes,
since they alone can never destroy his dreams
of finding some contentment here on earth.
Happy is he who, far from home, embraces
nothing but his long-lost memories,
because when new problems arise, he sees
them clearly, comprehending the sorrow he faces.
And happy is he who lives in *any* state
where only fraud and love's deceits and doubt,
are able to torture his heart from within.
But tragic is he who lives beneath the weight
of some unforgivable act, living without
full consciousness of the damages of his sin.

Nature

Luís de Camões
(Portuguese, 1524–1580)

The beauty of the sweet, fresh mountains here,
the shade of the green chestnut trees, the pace
of all the gently crawling streams, this place
where all one's sadness seems to disappear.
The hoarse soundings of the sea, the lands that lie
below, the sun hiding near the hills, the last
of the lingering cattle slowly moving past,
the clouds still gently warring in the sky.
But, finally, all these beauties of nature, pouring
forth their various splendors, only create
harsh fresh wounds since you're not here with me.
Without you, everything is disgusting and boring,
without you, I feel, even within this great
natural happiness, the greatest possible misery.

Refuge

Luís de Camões
(Portuguese, 1524–1580)

You who seek serenity in the wide
tempestuous sea of the world, cease
and abandon all hope of ever finding peace,
except in Jesus Christ, God Crucified.
If wealth absorbs your thoughts and preoccupies
your nights, God is the greatest treasure of all;
If you're looking for beauty, always recall
that God alone is the Beauty that satisfies.
If you seek delights to set your heart on fire,
remember that God's the sweetest of all, Who rewards
His followers with victory at last;
If honor and glory are what you most desire,
no greater honor or glory has ever surpassed
humbly serving the highest Lord of Lords.

Drowned Lover

Luís de Camões
(Portuguese, 1524–1580)

Dearest enemy, so often unkind,
my life was in your hands, until that wave
of the sea deprived you of an earthly grave,
depriving me, as well, of peace of mind.
The selfish drowning waters keep us apart,
enjoying your lovely beauty within the vast
cold sea, but as long as my broken life will last,
you'll always be alive within my heart.
And if my ragged poems can last for long
enough, your love, so spotless, will persist
forever and ever, as I, on your behalf,
will praise you always with my singing song;
as long as human memories exist,
my poems will be your missing epitaph.

Reader

Luís de Camões
(Portuguese, 1524–1580)

As long as Fortune dangled in my sight
the hope of happiness, my wishful schemes
for lasting love and all my youthful dreams
compelled me to lift my pen and write.
But Love, afraid I might prove indiscreet
and reveal her unpleasant truth, ingeniously
obscured my mind and cruelly tormented me,
trying to keep my pen from exposing her deceit.
But *you*, whom Love has also subjugated
to her fickle will, if you should come across
my verses, this little book of diverse
songs, conceived in experience, created
in truth, remember: the more you've loved and lost,
the better you'll comprehend my verse.

V. *The Ballad Rode into Town* (2007)

The Ballad Rode into Town

The ballad rode into town one day,
wearing his deadly gun,
and his Mexican spurs jingled along
in the heat of the mid-day sun.

He wore his blacks, he wore his boots,
he wore a Colt on his hip,
with a re-bored barrel, the trigger filed,
and a custom black-butt grip.

He'd come across the desert heats,
like Dante through his hell,
over the mesas, day and night,
through the sage and the chaparral.

Right up the only street in town,
he and his Morgan came,
as the free-verse rummies scattered,
and slithered away in shame.

But at the saloon, the rondels came out,
with the pretty villanelle,
"Now, *that's* what I would call a man —
a man with a story to tell."

And even the gambler couplet agreed,
"That's a mighty heroic chap,
who'll face them alone, and fire his Colt,
with the crack of a thunderclap."

They followed him past the Sheriff's door,
abandoned back in June,
then passed the burned-out *Weekly Press*,
in the silent afternoon.

The ballad rode into town that day,
wearing his deadly gun,
and his Mexican spurs jingled along
in the heat of the mid-day sun.

He rode his Morgan up the street,
and stopped at the only birch,
where all the decent blank-verse folk
were coming out of church.

"Where is she?" he said and waited,
under the Texas skies.
"I'm here!" the lovely sonnet called,
and lit up the rider's eyes.

"They've terrorized this western town,
and bullied us all, my dear.
So set things right and proper,
then take me away from here."

Right then, the critics gang rode up,
a motley crew of thugs,
with .38s and rifles cocked
with lethal dum-dum slugs.

Quickly, the fearful crowd dispersed,
to hide and watch and wait;

the gang boss sneered, "Any last words?"
as he aimed his .38.

But the ballad blew a bullet hole
right through the de-con's eye,
and dropped the freud and marxist crits,
and then the gender guy.

There were, when his chambers were empty,
six dead in the Texas heat;
there were, when he holstered his .45,
six thugs on the dusty street.

And when the celebration peaked,
Miss Sonnet reappeared,
and she and her man rode off to the west,
and even the rummies cheered.

So the ballad rode out of town that day,
still wearing his deadly gun,
and his Mexican spurs jingled along
in the heat of the mid-day sun.

Amnesiac

They found him in an alleyway
lying in the Delta heat,
concussed, unconscious, nearly dead,
not far from Bourbon Street.

Thirty-or-so, nicely-dressed,
he couldn't remember a thing;
he had no wallet, no watch, no scars,
and he had no wedding ring.

His past was a blackish empty pit,
"Who *am* I?" he asked the nurse.
"Someone who needs a lot of rest,
or things could get much worse."

But no one called the Nightly News
when they flashed his handsome face,
and his fingerprints drew a blank
in the federal database.

Trauma to the temporal lobe,
which would, of course, explain
the retrograde amnesia
in the cortex of the brain.

She read about him on the web —
amnesia.com.
She quit her job, and packed her car,
and hummed the 13th Psalm.

She drove from Vaughn to New Orleans,
planning their rendezvous,
then bumped his arm in Jackson Square,
"Excuse me, how are you?"

She looked into his pastless eyes,
he looked back vis-à-vis,
as then they promptly fell in love,
as prompt as prompt could be.

Three months later, they sat in the square,
thinking that love is blind,
"You always understand me, love,
but there's something on my mind.

"I've wondered," he said, "if we've met before,
back in my previous life,
and, more than once, I've wondered as well
if you're my loving wife?"

She smelled the white magnolias,
and felt the river breeze;
she looked at the French cathedral
and heard the rustling trees.

"Two years ago, and this is the truth,
and what I've left unsaid,
they found me on a Tulsa street,
and thought that I was dead.

"I woke in the county hospital,
but nothing was ever the same,

my past was a blank and empty pit,
and I couldn't remember my name.

"I've got no memories — not a one —
no mom, no dad, no sis,
I never went to church or school,
I never got a kiss.

"I have no friends to call at night,
I've got no favorite song,
I've had no plans, no hopes, no goals,
until you came along.

"And now that I've finally found you, love,
I want the present to last,
but I fear that hellish yawning pit,
and I hate the filthy past."

"But, dearest love, the past is past;
the wife I want is you!"
He flashed a brand-new diamond ring,
she smiled and said, "I do!"

They held each other contentedly
within the falling light,
then rose together arm-in-arm
and walked through the Delta night.

Not hearing the footsteps, subtle and soft,
that followed them through the park,
the ever-patient ominous past
creeping along in the dark.

The Ballad of the Labyrinths

after Borges

In Babylon, a mighty Shah
spent over a thousand days
building his "Wonder of the World,"
his inescapable maze.

With endless, dead-end corridors,
baffling walls and floors,
perplexing stairs and balustrades
misleading gates and doors.

A mystifying "created" world,
deceptive and inhumane,
too clever and too blasphemous,
self-satisfied, and vain.

Now when the King of Arabia
traveled north and east,
the Shah offered his simple guest
an honorary feast.

He showed him the palace, the dancing girls,
his jewel-encrusted throne,
then took his guest to the labyrinth
and left him all alone.

Where all night long, beneath the stars,
hour after hour,
the helpless king wandered the maze,
as the Shah watched from his tower.

While down below, the weary king
fell in a deep despair;
humiliated and confused,
he sank to his knees in prayer.

At dawn, he found the exit door,
at the sound of the morning bell,
but vowed that he would never discuss
his previous night in hell.

So when, at last, his host arrived,
he calmly offered his hand,
"I hope, someday, to show you, Shah,
a maze in my native land."

He then returned to Arabia,
amassing his wild forces:
a hundred thousand Bedouin riders
on fresh Arabian horses.

He nodded to his Dervishes,
and his army thundered forth,
with shrieks and cries and pounding hooves
into the Persian north.

Routing armies, sacking cities,
with calculated malice,
they crossed Najaf to Babylon
and burned the empty palace.

But the clever king of Arabia
knew where the Shah would hide,

so he ripped apart the labyrinth
and found the man inside.

Blindfolded, the Shah was put on a camel
and sipped the drugged-up wine
and heard the king of Arabia say,
"Now I can show you mine."

They rode through sweltering, southern heats
for nine relentless days,
until, at last, he fell asleep
in a suffocating haze.

When he awoke, with burning eyes,
from the darkness of his nap,
he sat on the ground in the blinding sun
with a parchment on his lap.

"Here, good Shah, is our southern maze,
where you are now set free,
built by God and nature, and called
the Rub' al Khali.

"It has no walls or passageways,
so may you fare-you-well,
though it's, by far, more intricate
than the labyrinths of hell."

Alone, the desperate Shah looked up,
to see his life was done,
trapped in the desert's burning sand,
beneath the flaming sun.

The Ballad of the Death-Row Lover

One night at Church by the Jersey Shore,
the day the Lord was risen,
Sweet Lee explained how they could soothe
the souls in Rahway Prison.

"We'll write them letters," said eager Sweet Lee
(who really was rather plain),
and pretty Jen concurred and said,
"Death row's so inhumane!"

To Jen the notion of capital crime
was totally unfair,
and she opposed the needle, the noose,
and the sparking electric chair.

"Dear Whistling Jack, I hope you're well,
and hope you'll enjoy my note.
And, yes, I know you had a wife,
before you slit her throat."

Back and forth, the letters flew
from spring to summertime;
they fell in love, and Jen believed,
"He's innocent of the crime."

"But I'll never send my photo," she sighed,
"off to that terrible place.

I want him to love the 'me' within,
and not my pretty face."

The kindly judges of the Garden State
issued a proclamation:
"Whistling Jack, on a legal point,
goes back in the population."

But still Jen needed to test his love,
and she asked her friend Sweet Lee,
"Would *you* meet Jack at the prison gates,
and pretend that you are me?"

The day that Jack was finally released,
she waited by the phone,
which didn't ring, and didn't ring,
but left her all alone.

"We've fallen in love," Sweet Lee explained,
"and we won't be coming back."
Jen smashed the phone against the wall,
"Now let me speak to Jack."

"But I'm the one who wrote the letters!"
"Who cares?" her lover said.
"Besides, I've got a pretty face!"
"Who cares?" The line went dead.

She swooned a week, then opened the *Post*,
and read the Coroner's quote:
"Whistling Jack took Missy Lee
and slit her naked throat."

The doorbell rang, she was in the kitchen,
praying her lunchtime grace.
She opened the door, Jack smiled and said,
"My, what a pretty face!"

Jack stepped inside, looked her up-and-down,
very much impressed,
but she thumped him with a carving knife,
deep in his cheating chest.

There was blood on the rug, blood on the walls,
blood all over the place.
There was blood on her dress, and her shaking hands,
and blood on her pretty face.

But now that he's gone, she still won't condone
the taking of human life,
with needles, or nooses, or electric chairs,
just with the carving knife.

VI. *"Bocage" and Other Sonnets* (2008)

Arrhythmia

He shouldn't, but he does. He runs up hills,
thinking about her inaccessibility,
her vanishings, her panics, and her pills,
and her ever-constant instability.
He stops at Dyson's summit, staring out
over the edge at the alien world below,
aware there's just one thing he cares about:
Where is she now? And *why* did she go?
He feels his pounding, racing, skipping heart,
its whirling tachycardia, its death-
like S.V.T.s, its sudden off-the-chart
fibrillation, and his paucity of breath.
He weakens in a wild, dizzying blur,
which feels just fine, because it feels like her.

Elevator

We shudder to a sudden crashing stop;
I stare at him as he looks back at me,
suspended above a thirty-story drop,
as calm in our business suits as calm can be.
We talk the market, sports, even our fears,
and once, lovingly, he mentions his wife,
never suspecting that she was my lover for years,
before she left for him, destroying my life.
A sudden bump-then-scrape jolts us hard,
then down we glide, hundreds of feet below.
In the lobby, he hands me his business card,
I give him a bogus name, then watch him go,
thinking of her, her scent, her touch, her voice,
but certain now, she's made the better choice.

Cartographer

(d. 1863)

On every Brazilian map of the Amazon,
thirteen miles south of São Miguel,
above the Amor basin, you'll come upon
the tiny tropic town of Isabel.
But if you *really* travel to the place,
there's nothing there; there's nothing there
at all, but swamp, and sun, and maybe just a trace
of wind that whispers her name in the sultry air.
Because these maps descend from those once drawn
by Tôrres, the master, who clearly understood,
when he awoke alone in his tent at dawn,
that Isabel had run away for good,
so he would mark his cartographic lie,
and mark her name, forever, and call goodbye.

Wanted Poster

He checks the poster-wall and finds his own:
"Caution." "Wanted by the F.B.I."
It's just a sketch, his "whereabouts unknown,"
it lists no name, address, or reasons "why."
Mesmerized, he stares into his face,
which moves him deeply, even, almost to tears,
it seems so human, so full of warmth and grace.
He shudders. He hasn't felt this good in years.
He thinks about the artist, whoever, wherever,
she is, who seems to understand, forgive.
He wants to thank her, maybe even forever.
Why not track her down. Where does she live?
Maybe it's time for a visit? A rendezvous?
When you're on the lam, there's nothing else to do.

Fog

On the densest days, he guides his little boat
into the heart of the fog, turns off the key,
lies on the deck, and lets it float,
drifting sightless over the gentle sea,
into that all-consuming whitish-grey
of the fog, into its palpable negation,
into its wets and damps, drifting away
into its gradual world of obliteration,
where nothing-at-all exists except
the solipsism, which, in time, will bring
to him the essence of himself: swept-
away, a blank, devoid of everything,
except the thought of you, and of your death,
enshrouded in mist as moist as your final breath.

Intruder

For hours, you watch her sleep. Sitting close by,
in a shaft of light, in the scent of her perfume.
Breaking-in was easy, with the moonlit sky,
her husband away, and the kids asleep in their room.
Twelve years ago, your love went south, went bust,
she called it off. But she's got nothing to fear,
there's no venom in your heart, no lust,
no bitterness. No, *that*'s not why you're here.
Remember the time she shut her lovely eyes,
asleep in your arms, after that bottle of wine?
She stirs, shifts in her bed, and sighs,
but you're unconcerned, you're feeling fine.
You rise, you block the light, her bed goes black,
you whisper something, leave, and never come back.

Self-Portrait

Manuel du Bocage
(Portuguese, 1765–1805)

Thin, darkly-complected, and medium-tall,
solid on my feet, with eyes of blue,
sad-faced, with a sadish appearance too,
and a nose that's uppity and not-too-small.
Unable to stay in one place, inclined to aggressions,
rage, unkindness, often lifting up
with innocent hands the darkest cup
and drinking the venom of my lethal, hellish obsessions.
The worshipper of a thousand gods. (I've lied:
a thousand girls.) Loving them even before
the sacred altars where the friars pray.
Such is Bocage, in whom some talents reside,
who was struck with all these truths and more,
while he was lounging around one day.

Camões

Manuel du Bocage
(Portuguese, 1765–1805)

Camões, how similar, great master,
I find your fate to mine. We both once found
ourselves sailing away from the Tagus, bound
for the East, to face the sea-god Adamastor.
Like you, at the murmuring Ganges, I sit in the mire
of terrible destitutions and endless terrors;
Like you, with your foolish pleasures and lusty errors,
I'm also the wistful lover of useless desire.
Scornful, like you, of all my bad luck, I grow
despondent, praying for some certainty that might create
some peace in the grave whenever my life is through.
You've been my mentor. But, sadly, even though
I've imitated you in the sensualities of fate,
I've never, in the arts, been able to emulate you.

Inês de Castro

(Murdered 1/7/1355)

Manuel du Bocage
(Portuguese, 1765–1805)

The sad and beautiful Inês, recalling that day,
cries out her tearful echo, which, always repeating,
begs the merciful heavens for justice, entreating
against the assassins who stole her life away.
Her cries are heard at the Fountain of Love in the hours
when the lovely water-nymphs grieve and pray,
where the Mondego, recalling that infamous day,
angrily floods its banks and drowns its flowers.
The universe, itself, offers hymns above
for Pedro, the Prince, who learns of her death and races
to his love, who lies in her grave, to exhume
that miracle of beauty, kindness, and love.
Who opens, beholds, kneels, groans, and embraces;
then crowns his ill-fated Inês within her tomb.

Letter of Resignation

Dear [blank]: After much deliberation,
without qualm, scruple, or further delay,
I hereby tender my formal resignation
as your lover and future fiancé.
The job provides too little satisfaction:
too many hours of unneeded duress,
a paucity of productive interaction,
uncertain working conditions, and endless stress.
Pay-wise, I'm undervalued and disenchanted:
advancement's slow, the bonus is routine,
my "on-call" overtime is taken for granted,
and benefits are few and far between.
This document, I'm hopeful, underscores
my deep regret. I'm very truly yours . . .

Impersonator

I've been a congressman, a film producer,
a big-time novelist, a New Age quack,
a Kennedy, a Grammy introducer,
a Fox reporter, an all-pro cornerback.
Sure, it's fraud, but I've lived at the Ritz,
cruised Hawaii and the Maritimes,
done the Oscars, comped the glitz
in Vegas, and been to La Scala six times.
Dangerous? I've been arrested at least
five times and never spent a night in jail.
But it's not easy. It takes a true *artiste*,
absolute commitment, refusal to fail,
and far more talent than any of those fad-
ish money-grubbing celebrities ever had.

Chocolate

Why did Montezuma give his guest,
Hernán Cortés, that rather bitter "tea"
his Aztec farmers had carefully pressed
from the tropical seeds of the cacao tree?
And why did the Dominican friars bring
it back to Spain, from where, by chance,
the young María, engaged to the Bourbon King,
would introduce the "sweetened" drink to France?
And why, from London, did Mr. Fry present
to the waiting world the "chocolate bar," well worth
its weight in gold, and why did Nestlé invent
"milk" chocolate, the greatest thing on earth?
To please, of course, my love, watching her DVR,
emparadised, eating her chocolate bar.

Protanopia

The Tate Gallery

He stood in the palace of color, colorblind,
surrounded by Rossetti, Hunt, and John Millais,
yet in the visual cortex of his mind,
their pinks were blue, their reds were black and gray.
His worthless retinal cones were still immune
to color brightness — permanent, severe,
congenital — but then she entered the room
and colored his world like Morris' *Guinevere*.
He now could see the reddest crimson red,
and peacock, ruby, pink, and apricot.
"I don't know who or what you are?" he said.
"The cure," she answered with a smile. "For what?"
Then, drenched with color in the Pre-Raph wing,
she whispered in black-and-white: "Everything!"

Like a Speeding Bullet

She comes in like a speeding bullet, a ticker-
tape parade, a cardiac,
a Kansas twister, SWAT, 100-proof liquor,
a 4-alarm, and an aphrodisiac.
She whirls into a fog, an acid trip,
a dust storm, a kaleidoscope,
a question mark, a busted microchip,
quicksand, an unmailed envelope.
She leaves you like a shipwreck, a TKO,
roadkill, a 911, a windshield bug,
a popped balloon, a spilt Merlot,
a spent shell-casing lying on the rug,
thinking, "Hey, I love her, *whatever* she does,
just give me more of whatever that was!"

The Rain Rains

Cecília Meireles
(Brazilian, 1901–1964)

The rain falls gently like a silent sleep
that calms and tranquilizes. The rain
rains down with abandon. The rains sweep
down with the musical poetry of Verlaine,
which conjures a dream of a gloomy Halloween
and a certain timeless, abandoned palace
which evokes, in the vespers, the lyric and unseen
things of autumn, which poison the soul with malice.
Within that distant ancient palace, in that strange
and far-off land, in that misty mountain range,
the organs play moribund arias that murmur along
the huge and ghastly corridors, with the wind whipping
beneath the cracks of doors and flipping
the pages of missals, tomes, and books of song.

Spider Hole

Cecília Meireles
(Brazilian, 1901–1964)

Up where even the dust can't reach that high,
she weaves her fragile web, to and fro,
then quickly back and forth, by and by,
without fatigue, mistake, or vertigo.
And when she's done her work, her very best,
she then reveals her magnificent web; then free
at last, the little spider takes her rest,
surrounded by her silken majesty.
The fires of the voluptuous sun ignite
her web, as she sits at its center, a gemstone,
like a glittering tawny topaz, and I believe
this spider is a philosopher, a bright
deserter from the world, all alone,
entangled in the subtle dreams she weaves.

Coimbra Night

Cecília Meireles
(Brazilian, 1901–1964)

Enchanted night! Everything is white,
as though bathed in the pallor of opal. With lulling ease,
the Mondego River seems to fall asleep tonight
and dream beneath the caressing sighs of the breeze.
Tonight, warm with love, everything's at rest,
and yet, the silvery moon wishes it knew
why it's uneasy, why it's distressed,
why it's languid and cold in the faded blue.
In the garden of the sleeping palace, where
the serenading nightingales sing
their love to the flowers, the moon paints everything white,
while, near the fountain, in the sighs of someone there
who's conjured the dead: Pedro, the son of the king,
kisses Inês de Castro within the Coimbra night.

Cage

He hears her rattling the bars of the cage
(their love) like a shattering deafening drum.
The whole house pulsates with her frustrated rage.
Surely the neighbors will call. The cops will come.
His head is throbbing; he needs to get away.
He steps outside, trying to decompress:
What is his perfect lover trying to say?
Does she need something *else*? Or *more*? Or *less*?
They'd built their lovers' cage with such precision
and mutuality. They were so clever,
calmly discussing every single decision,
building the bloody thing to last forever.
He enters the little chapel, sits in the cold,
and prays and prays the bars will hold.

Bookstore

The “celebrity” memoir was moving fast,
a *Times* bestseller. She opened a copy and checked
the index for her names, both first and last.
Neither was there. What did she expect?
That he’d remember Lisbon from years ago,
their weeks in Casçais, their lovers’ pirouette?
That he’d lament the one who’d told him, “No,”
that she’d, somehow, still be his “one regret”?
She put the book back down, and left the store,
then calmly got in her car, heading uptown,
never reading in chapter twenty-four
about “Marie” in quotes, who’d “turned him down,”
who was his “only, ever, perfect love,”
whom he was “still and always” thinking of.

The Shower

"Younger than springtime," she sings, fading
in and out, for nearly a half an hour,
always the love songs, with the water cascading
over her lovely nakedness in the shower.
She's dead, of course. It's just a tape he'd made
on a lark, sixteen years ago, as she howled away
like an angel in their bathroom. And now, he played
it every morning, the best part of his day.
Sometimes he'd sing along and pathetically dream
that she was still alive, that everything was all right,
that soon she'd open the door, in the billowing steam,
and towel herself off in the early morning light.
But then, the tape fades out, clicks, yet doesn't break,
just hisses hisses like a rattlesnake.

The Puzzle House

"I think you think I don't know who you are,"
she says at the window, "but I know what I know."
She sits across her tiny, white, bizarre,
and sterile room, watching the falling snow.
He stares at the half-done puzzle on the floor:
Escher's *Waterfall,* just more confusions
for someone seldom coherent anymore,
being "aphasic" with monothematic delusions.
But now her stabilizers, clozapine,
and stimulants ignite some hope. She tries
to peer beyond the smothering routine:
"It's like a puzzle!" She looks into his eyes,
but fails. She doesn't have a clue:
"Where do *you* fit in? Which piece are you?"

Illiterate Love Note

It lay on his desk: "Do you no how I feel?
I love you more and still yet more. Your frend."
He picked it up. How odd. Even surreal.
He read it again, trying to comprehend.
It was that pretty immigrant girl, Yvonne,
who cleaned his office every Wednesday night,
when he'd stay late and they'd talk on and on,
right through her breaks, into the morning light.
Did she know he craved to love her in every way?
That he dreamed of marrying her? That when he died,
after loving her every night and day,
he'd have, within his coffin box, inside
the inside-pocket of his funeral coat,
over his heart, this marvelous perfect note?

The “2” Train

116th & Lennox

Suppose you wake to a Bossa Nova song
somewhere in Spanish Harlem near the park;
suppose you sit in your bed and sing along,
watching the dawn fuss away the dark.
Suppose you rise, undress yourself, and shower,
staring into the mirrors (unaware
how lovely you are), then spend another hour,
choosing your bright red dress and combing your hair.
Suppose you catch the train, like you always do,
to rumble underground for fifty blocks,
but suppose, today, the man across from you
is writing this poem on the top of a small white box.
Suppose he rises, holding a red red rose,
leans over, smiles, and says to you, “Suppose . . . .”

VII. *Psalter*
(2011)

Snake

Genesis 3:5

Yes, you have a lovely garden here,
with flowers, fields and fruits, lakes and streams,
beneath a Tree of Life, with nothing to fear,
in a paradise of pleasure, a place of dreams.
And, yes, you have each other's trust and love,
naked, as if one flesh, chaste and free;
and, yes, you have dominion, over and above,
everything as far as the eye can see.
And yet, you lack a certain acuity,
a comprehension of all that lies within,
of good, of evil, of ambiguity,
of death, and of the leprosy of sin.
Become as gods, transform to something new;
put hiss in your voice and fork your tongue in two.

Pharaoh

Exodus 10:22

I breathe the blackness of perpetuant night,
where nothing is seen, where nothing can be done,
where darkness obliterates every trace of light:
"What kind of god can blot away the sun?"
Three days ago, when Moses cast his spell,
the locusts whirled into the seas forever,
but when I stood my ground, the blackness fell.
No matter, I'll never capitulate. *Never.*
"Father?" I hear a frightened voice. "I'm here."
Unseen, my little boy, the eldest one,
comes forth, and sensing my child's fear,
I pull him close and tightly hold my son,
thinking, within our obsidian abyss,
"Surely, *nothing* could be worse than this."

David

I Kings 24:1

The putrid sea lies right beneath my cave,
its stinking rising sulfur burns my eyes,
for nothing can survive this smoldering grave,
where every bird and plant and creature dies,
where even the valleys and the hills are dead;
for this is "desolation," a world apart,
with Sodom's Mountain looming straight ahead,
where all is dark and barren like my heart.
Lord, help me in my lonely, useless life,
hunted by the king, like a treacherous slave,
without my friends, my brothers, or my wife,
just waiting to be slaughtered in my cave.
O Lord, I know not what to do,
so in this valley of death I turn to You.

Elijah

III Kings 19:12

After forty days and forty nights,
Elijah, beneath a dark and ominous sky,
arrives at Sinai, ascending to its heights,
in total despair, wishing he could die.
Then the wind comes, like an epitaph,
its whirling gusts begin to ravage and swarm
and batter the world and break its rocks in half.
But God is *not* in the wind of the storm.
Then the earth quakes, and the world begins to sway,
even the mountain seems to shatter and break.
Then the fire comes, blazing the world away.
But God is *not* in the flames, *not* in the quake.
Then, there's but a whisper in the air,
the small still voice of love. And God is there.

Jezebel

IV Kings 9:36

"How beautiful I am!" thinks Jezebel,
whose scented sensuous skin is beyond compare,
who wears luxurious robes in her citadel,
with colored eyes and lush Phoenician hair.
Then Jehu, the "avenger," rides up and calls
to her willing pagan eunuchs: "Throw her down!"
where crushed by horses, her blood sprays on the walls,
her flesh attracting the dogs that scavenge the town.
Then Jehu says, it's as Elijah said,
who described the fate that the Lord had said would be:
that dogs would eat the scented flesh of the dead,
and those who passed-on-by would see
the dog dung in the field and smell the smell
and ask: "Is that the beauty Jezebel?"

Jeremiah

Lamentations 3:16

In the smoldering ashes of Zion, I sit alone
in smoke, in bitterness, woodworm, and gall;
I suffocate within the dust and moan
for the once-great city I knew was destined to fall.
The Babylonians came without pity;
they busted the walls, and then, before they were gone,
they wrecked the temple and burned the holy city,
then took my people into Babylon,
who worshipped foreign idols, tempting the Lord,
and now lay rotting without their proper graves,
slaughtered by the might of the pagan sword;
their women defiled, now dead or helpless slaves.
And yet, despite what Zion has become,
I sit in the ashes and wait for Him-to-come.

Theotokos

Luke 1:38

Before eternity, in spaceless space,
in timelessness, in time before all-time,
the mind of God, with enigmatic grace,
conceived the Panagia, the paradigm,
the goal of generative history,
the masterpiece, of whom God said
that she and her seed, that fathomless mystery,
would crush the serpent's bloody head.
Who seemed an obscure Jewish girl until
that moment-of-moments when she would say:
"*Fiat*," the handmaid of her Father's will,
to consummate eternity, then pray,
humbly accepting she-knows-not-what,
singing her silent Magnificat.

Egypt

Matthew 2:14

I watch them sleep in the flickering firelight
beneath the pyramids of this alien land.
Watching, I'm ready for anything tonight,
beneath the stars in this ever-cooling sand.
At least, for now, they're safe from Herod's wrath.
We left, when the angel came, without a trace
and followed God's strange path, His only path,
into this lonely, heathen desert place.
Still alert, I take a moment to pray,
then hear a sudden threatening sound from the east;
the child stirs, but the noise then fades away.
It's clear there's no real danger, for now, at least,
as Mary smiles and sings to calm our fears
a song that seems the music of the spheres.

Centurion

Matthew 2:16

I've slaughtered babies all day long,
near Bethlehem. But why? If the wizards are right,
nothing can alter the Fates, and, if they're wrong,
we're killing without a reason. So now, at night,
I wash the dry and splattered blood away,
then fall to sleep, into a feverish hell,
hearing the wails of the mothers as they pray
for retribution and vengeance, hearing, as well,
my mother's voice — who nursed me through the sweats
when I was born — whose melodious words now sing,
above the whirl of curses and alien threats:
"Whoever injures a child is a fiendish thing,"
whispering, like Rachel, not so long ago,
"and lower than the lowest of the low."

Andrew

Mark 1:17

I well remember that we'd just begun
to cast our fishing nets into the sea,
and then I saw him, in the mid-day sun,
standing there before us in Galilee.
Behold the One the Baptist bows before!
The one he calls the Lamb who'll set us free!
Then Jesus looked at us from the shore,
we fishers of fish, and said, "Follow me."
Immediately, I dropped my heavy net,
and everything I had in Galilee,
and leapt out from the boat, without regret,
not even thinking what my future might be,
not even thinking, what could He possibly see
in a sweaty ignorant fisherman like me?

Love Your Enemies

Matthew 5:44

Did he *really* say that? *Never* despise
your enemies? Give love to those who hate,
who injure, sabotage, and vandalize,
who curse, demean us, and humiliate?
Yes, he's turning the world upside-down:
no "eye for an eye," but "blessed are the meek"
who fortify themselves with grace to drown
their angry rage and turn the other cheek.
"Love your enemies," commandeth the Lord.
Don't plot against them, hate, or condemn,
for human vengeance merits no reward.
Instead, do good to them. And pray for them.
And love them in your pains, in your disgrace,
even when they spit into your face.

Light of the World

John 8:12

Not as the candle luminates the room,
nor even as the sun illumes the day,
but as, into the blackness of the tomb,
into its feculence and foul decay,
there lights, upon the lifeless eyes of those,
imprisoned there, in sin and self-disgust,
who sweat, and fear, and weep, and decompose,
each day, into the vile putrid dust:
a blazing luminescent shaft of light,
that bedazzles the minds of those who sit
within the hopeless darkness of the night,
revealing a passage away from the festering pit,
leading, at last, through grace, through sacrifice,
into the luminescence of paradise.

VIII. *Love Sonnets* (2016)

Itinerary

"How Many People Have Lived on Earth?"
107,602,707,791
— Population Reference Bureau

You're sitting on a rock, hurtling along
at 2.7 million m.p.h. (or more),
within a sea of stars, a billion strong,
zipping towards some stupid "galactic core."
But your itinerary's nothing but gaps.
You sit atop your little blue-ish sphere,
just like the other 100 billion saps,
and wonder, "What the hell am I doing here?"
Until you see her, later in the day,
strolling up Fordham Road, as if she knew
that you were watching, as if to say,
"I give purpose to everything I do,"
wearing a tight black sweater in the September breeze,
and tight to-die-for bright-white dungarees.

Island Beach

You emerge from the waves, unexpectedly alone,
more lovely than Venus rising from the sea,
on the most important day I've ever known,
into whatever, inexplicably, might-be,
dripping wet in your yellow bathing suit,
so heartstoppingly beautiful I never even asked why
everything else in my life is suddenly moot,
beneath the Jersey sun and the summer sky.
And what preposterous unthinking youthful pride
made me think you'd stop at the dunes, at the piers,
and look at *me*, still staring, mystified,
and become the love who eliminates all my fears?
Except, of course, the one I can never forget:
the unfounded fear that we might never have met.

Sappy Love Poem

The poets, who used to think otherwise,
will read this sonnet, scoff and snipe,
call it embarrassing, and roll their eyes
at its mushy, low-brow, sentimental tripe.
Well, the hell with them! What do I care?
When you still "walk in beauty" every night,
the moonlight in your eyes and windswept hair,
the inexplicable "phantom" of my delight;
when you're the *only* thing I'm thinking of,
in the city, the bedroom, or on the beach,
where we've confabulated this hyper-love
with "two hearts beating each to each,"
whose hearts still jump when the other enters the room,
thump-thump-thump, and, yes, boom-boom-boom.

Lying in Bed with Me

I love you standing near the fireplace
in your little black Coco Chanel,
or dressed in your uniform at second base,
or hailing a cab with a bottle of Zinfandel.
I love you walking the beach at Barnegat Light,
or strolling the aisles of the grocery store,
or barefoot in the clover fields at night,
or up the steps and through the cathedral door.
I love you sitting asleep in your library chair,
or watching a western at the Paradise,
or sitting in your boudoir combing your hair,
or dining at Vinni's with a pizza slice.
I love you lying in your hammock sipping tea,
or, best of all, lying in bed with me.

Bad Girl Sonnet: Redux

Yeah, Baby drives with the headlights off at night,
with a bottle of cherry Ripple in her lap,
and sings: "I'm a stinkin' stick of dynamite!
My fuse is lit, and I don't give a crap!"
Yeah, she won't get off the rides at the Jersey shore;
she stands on her chair and yells at the boxing matches;
she gets in fights, but always evens the score,
then shows up late with bruises, cuts, and scratches.
Yeah, she dangles her legs off the edge of the water tower,
gets taken to some dump for "screwed-up juveniles,"
then fights with the county shrink for over an hour.
When I show up, she takes my hand and smiles:
"Yeah, everyone thinks I'm crazy, which is true:
Sure, I'm crazy — *crazy* in love with you."

Bad Girl Sonnet: Hey, Good-Lookin'

Yeah, my pretty Baby wears nothing but black:
tight Wrangler jeans, unfaded, black, and dark,
and black T-shirts with writings on the back,
like "Vote for Nixon" or "Welcome to Asbury Park."
My Baby wears her hair in the page-boy style,
which always smells of coconut shampoo;
she wears a whiff of "Roses of the Nile"
and a ring engraved: "I Love You-Know-Who."
My Baby wears black leathers in the fall;
a pea coat when the snow swirls from the west.
Of course, I wish my Baby wore nothing at all,
but, short of that, the thing that I love best
is the smile she always wears whenever we meet,
whenever she sees me cruisin' up the street.

The Betrayal

It's never left. It's still inside this place,
under the rug, under the storage bin,
under the bed, under the pillowcase,
or maybe lurking beneath somebody's skin.
Maybe I should raze the place to the ground,
obliterating every single speck,
or take some gasoline, spread it around,
and torch this dump into a smoldering wreck?
But I need to find it. I need to remember *why*,
and *who* did *what* to *whom*, and end all doubt;
I need to look it firmly in the eye.
Even though, the *only* thing I'm certain about
is that, whenever I find its hiding place,
it'll have a smirk on its leering ugly face.

Dry-Rot

By chance, you see him in the new café
sitting in some cozy one-on-one
with someone new. "So what?" your friends will say,
"Everyone knows you two are over and done."
Yet within your inner inner-self, of course,
you're overwhelmed with a devastating flood
of useless memories, regret, remorse,
and, yes, a desperate longing in the blood.
Just like that flood in Texas years ago
that ravaged everything that it embraced,
and even after the pumps reversed its flow,
it left a filthy toxic ring of waste
three-feet high in all the rooms and halls,
and left its stinking dry-rot in the walls.

Toxicity

The deadliest toxin yet classified,
Batrachotoxin, more deadly than primal sin,
worse than arsenic, curare, and cyanide,
excretes from the dart frog's poison skin.
As for acids, if you check the science books,
the most corrosive acid ever known
is Fluoroantimonic Acid, which looks
like water, yet dissolves both skin and bone.
But a toxin, even more deadly and destructive,
as everyone knows (or will soon discover),
is the sweet, delicious, and seductive
scalding moisture on the lips of your lover,
who, without telling you exactly why,
leans close to you and kisses you goodbye.

ICU

Some moron cuts me off on the Garden State,
not too far from the exit for Route 22;
I crash the retaining wall, wheel back too late,
flip over twice, and end in the ICU,
with a broken this-and-that, fibrillation,
a punctured something, spinal repercussion,
intravenous morphine medication,
with an almost-deadly brain concussion.
But now I'm thinking *maybe* it's not so bad,
maybe you'll hear about it and visit me,
as I sketch your face on a prescription pad,
dreaming of a moment that's never-to-be:
when I hear your footsteps on the hallway floor,
when I see you, love, coming through the door.

Embraceable You

How fortunate the darkness, which every night,
holds you and comforts your worries away;
how fortunate, each dawn, is the morning light,
with a touch that illumes and warms your day.
How fortunate is the water when you undress
and step within the liquids of the shower,
or sink to a soothing bath, within a caress
that holds you close for nearly an hour.
How fortunate even the invisible air,
which, like a lover who can do no wrong,
silently supports you everywhere,
gently embracing you all day long.
How unfortunate am I, who misses you,
wishing to hold you like I used to do.

Turbulence

Overall, it's been a pretty bumpy ride:
nothing but endless turbulent flights
into the vortices, banging from side to side,
staring helpless at the emergency lights.
Not to mention more than one crash-and-burn,
in which some pretty aviatrix would race
into chaotic skies, into a downward turn,
intentionally, with a smile on her face.
Until there was *you*. So lovely in your uniform
and captain's wings, the flawless aviator,
avoiding all convections, diffusions, and storms,
the perfect anti-turbulent navigator,
calmly doing whatever you need to do,
gliding us gently into the cerulean blue.

The Swimming Pool Float

He remembers, before she died last May,
watching as she slowly blew-up and inflated
that circular reddish float, puffing away,
as their eager little children waited.
He recalls her love, her yellow bathing suit,
that every breath we take in the summer breeze
contains some fifty million super-minute
molecules once breathed by Sophocles . . . .
Tonight, holding the float, when the night is cool,
he moves her chair to exactly the same place,
opens the valve, and sits beside the pool,
then feels her breath rush gently over his face,
alone with loneliness, alone with death,
he inhales her last remaining breath.

Meet Me in the Apocalypse

Who cares if it's a comet from outer space,
some eco-collapse, nukes, A.I. microchips,
or a viral pandemic destroying the human race:
Just come and meet me in the Apocalypse.
Just like that day I was playing third base
and saw you watching through the summer haze.
We talked about baseball, the tight pennant race,
Walter Johnson, Jeter, and Willie Mays.
We traded our caps, and you brushed back your hair,
"Meet me at the rapids at midnight tonight,"
and, of course, I would have met you anywhere,
which I did, and I kissed your lips in the soft moonlight.
Come, beneath the final, solar eclipse,
and meet me, my love, in the Apocalypse.

Love

I Corinthians 13:13

If I have not love, I'm but a hollow sound,
a tinkling cymbal destined to fade and fall,
and though my faith might move the mountains around,
still, without love, I'm nothing at all.
For love is patient, love is kind,
it's never vain, ambitious, or uncouth,
it's never coarse, it's soft, refined,
for love rejoices in the truth.
Love thinks no evil, it thinks no wrong,
it hopes, believes, endures, prevails,
love envieth not, it suffereth long,
it never turns, it never fails.
Have love, have faith, have hope, again and again,
but love is the greatest of these. Amen.

The Author:

William Baer, a recent Guggenheim fellow, is the author of twenty-three books, including six collections of poetry, most recently *Love Sonnets*. His various books include *"Bocage" and Other Sonnets* (recipient of the X.J. Kennedy Poetry Prize), *Luís de Camões: Selected Sonnets*; *Classic American Films: Conversations with the Screenwriters*; *Writing Metrical Poetry*; and *The Unfortunates* (recipient of the T.S. Eliot Award). A graduate of Rutgers and N.Y.U., he received his doctorate at the University of South Carolina under the direction of James Dickey. He also has graduate degrees from The Writing Seminars at Johns Hopkins and the School of Cinematic Arts at the University of Southern California. A former Fulbright (Portugal) and the recipient of a NEA Creative Writing Fellowship, he was the founding editor of *The Formalist* and currently serves as the contributing editor at *Measure*. He is also the author of two novels (*Companion* and *New Jersey Noir*) and two collections of short fiction (*Times Square and Other Stories* and *One-and-Twenty Tales*), and his various plays have been performed at over thirty American theaters.

Website: williambaer.net

www.ingramcontent.com/pod-product-compliance
Lightning Source LLC
Chambersburg PA
CBHW020611310726
48979CB00008B/1435/J

* 9 7 8 1 9 3 9 5 7 4 2 6 8 *